To my dear friend

Herbert Miller

William LaRoi. Jr

Oct. 9 - 53

THE CHURCH WE LOVE

WILBUR LA ROE, JR.

THE CHURCH WE LOVE

ABINGDON-COKESBURY PRESS
NEW YORK • NASHVILLE

THE CHURCH WE LOVE

Library of Congress Catalog Card Number: 53-10009

SET UP, PRINTED, AND BOUND BY THE
PARTHENON PRESS, AT NASHVILLE,
TENNESSEE, UNITED STATES OF AMERICA

To
the Christian laymen of America
with every good wish
and an earnest prayer

Preface

Nothing in my whole life of more than six decades has meant as much to me as the church. Many years ago I fell in love with the church, and the passing of the years has increased my love. So great is my obligation to the church that I feel under a duty to try to put into words what it has meant to me. For I long to have others get from the church what I have gotten and to be convinced, as I have been convinced, of the indispensability of Christ's gospel in dealing with the great issues confronting our world today. Only the church can save our Christian civilization. My great fear is that our Christian culture may be lost because of the inadequacy of our discipleship. Hence this book.

WILBUR LA ROE, JR.

Contents

1. In Earthen Vessels 11
2. Our Ministers 15
3. The Christian Layman 23
4. The Miracle of Life 31
5. The Abundant Life 36
6. Aiming at the Stars 40
7. Our Precious Heritage 43
8. Sacrificing for Love 47
9. When Trouble Comes 49
10. Missions 53
11. Prayer 57
12. Our Homes and Our Youth 61
13. Christian Friendship 68
14. The Church Music 71
15. Our Lord and Master 75

I love Thy Church, O God!
Her walls before Thee stand,
Dear as the apple of Thine eye,
And graven on Thy hand.

For her my tears shall fall,
For her my prayers ascend,
To her my cares and toils be given,
Till toils and cares shall end.

—Timothy Dwight

CHAPTER 1

In Earthen Vessels

"What we need is a burning and passionate faith."
—Elton Trueblood

Bill Jones was a hard customer to interest in the church. When we called on him, we found him reading the Sunday sports page with his feet propped up on a radiator. He did not get up to greet us, but shook hands with us indifferently from his half-reclining position.

No, thank you, he had lost interest in the church. He had had his fill of church in his early days, and he did not feel that he could stand any more of it. Anyway, he did not feel that the church was doing much good.

But today, only one and one-half years after our first visit, Bill Jones is an active member of our church and one of its loyal supporters.

What made the difference? The answer is simple: Two laymen made several calls on Bill, one of them invited him to lunch, another played golf with him, and the minister meanwhile did everything within his power to show a loving interest in him and in his family.

Bill Jones is typical of a multitude of men who have lost interest in the church because the church has lost interest in them. The sad fact is that one half of all church members are AWOL every Sunday, largely because they are neglected.

All over the United States, Christian laymen are awaking to the fact that conditions in our world are far too serious to allow any such condition to continue. A new spirit is stirring among our laymen. When President Eisenhower broke precedent by opening his inaugural address with prayer, and soon afterward joined the church, American laymen were thrilled.

President Eisenhower is by no means the only prominent citizen who is taking the church more seriously. Conrad Hilton, American hotel magnate and consecrated Christian layman, addressed a group of Christian laymen at a breakfast recently. Displaying a striking picture of Uncle Sam on his knees in prayer, Mr. Hilton warned the group that the world has lost its way and that we must get down on our knees and pray to almighty God for salvation. A few days later Attorney General Brownell, addressing a large group, said: "It is not enough to talk about brotherhood; we must talk about brotherhood *under God,* for we are all his children."

John Foster Dulles, now Secretary of State, appeals to his fellow Christian laymen with the argument that it is not enough merely to declare our Christian principles; we must get down into the public arena and fight for them. He is doing so himself.

J. Howard Pew, retired president of Sun Oil Company, devotes his entire time to serving his Lord, and he has received a citation from United Church Men for "distinguished lay service at the national level."

Governor Arthur Langlie of Washington travels all the way to Chicago to tell nearly two thousand Presbyterian delegates to take the church more seriously and to pray more than ever.

Senator Frank Carlson of Kansas is so concerned about the cause of Christ that he has accepted the chairmanship of a religious breakfast group which meets one morning each week in the United States Senate.

Paul Moser, a willing and tireless disciple, gave up a grocery business in Topeka, Kansas, and devotes his whole time to organizing Christian laymen for more effective work for Christ. He has already organized close to 100,000 laymen.

Tom Whiteman, a chain-store executive, and Lem T. Jones, a nationally known candy manufacturer in Kansas City, both consecrated laymen, are traveling thousands of miles to alert other laymen to the dangers confronting our nation and are urging them to pray.

Why this tremendous upsurge in Christian lay interest?

Why the unprecedented construction of new churches?

Why the organization of a great laymen's movement under the auspices of the United Council of Churches, headed by E. Urner Goodman, able and consecrated former leader of the Boy Scouts of America, who now spends all his time uniting the laymen of thirty denominations into a new army for Christ?

Why the rapidly expanding "Every Man Plan," initiated by a layman and aimed at giving every man in the church a significant part in the life and work of the church?[1]

Why the new interest in Christian missions and in Christian education?

The answer to these questions lies in the conviction of Christian men and women everywhere that the threats to our civilization, due to our lack of dependence on Christ, are extremely serious and that only the church can get our lost world back on its track. There is a new awareness

[1] The Every Man Plan is described on p. 29.

on the part of laymen of the fact that it is the gospel of Jesus Christ, and that gospel alone, that can provide an effective alternative to a totalitarian and godless ideology which already claims the allegiance of millions and which even now is enslaving whole nations. When Christian laymen take a fresh look at the gospel of Jesus Christ against the background of present-day Communism and fascism, they come to a new understanding of the relevancy of Jesus Christ and his gospel to the greatest issue confronting our world—the freedom and dignity of man. Regardless of political views, laymen are beginning to see clearly that no government can rightfully call itself Christian if it is the master of the people. The issue between Christian governments and non-Christian governments becomes clearer as church people grasp the awful significance of the Iron Curtain, which not only shuts out the free world but also shuts God out.

Too, laymen are becoming aware of the danger of a rampant secularism. They sense the danger in worshiping temporary gods. They note a new hunger among men everywhere for a sure foundation on which to build their lives. That foundation is Jesus Christ.

But there is another reason for the new lay interest. Prominent leaders of the church are, like the prophets of old, sounding a note of alarm. The church is being shaken out of its complacency by the thundering of many powerful and prophetic voices.

No warning is more grave than that of Dr. Charles Clayton Morrison, eminent Christian editor, who declares that Protestantism is lost among the great magnitudes of this day as Trinity Church is lost among the skyscrapers of Wall Street.

Elton Trueblood, one of the great religious thinkers of our day, refers to Christian laymen as mere "spectators in the church." Professor Norborg, writing in *Theology Today*, brings a still stronger indictment against laymen by describing them as "saltless," a truly offensive adjective to apply to disciples of Jesus Christ. Meanwhile, Dr. John A. Mackay, president of Princeton Theological Seminary, says that we Protestants have "a balcony religion," his implication being that, in a metaphorical sense, we sit on our comfortable Protestant church balconies and watch the crowds milling below, afraid to mingle with them lest we get our nice Protestant shoes dirty.

For the awful fact is that Jesus Christ is losing out in some of the vital areas of life. He is losing out in the international area as the two halves of the world hate and distrust each other. He is losing out in the area of government as states become the masters of their people, and as immorality reaches into high places. He is losing out in the American home as the holy bond of matrimony weakens and often breaks under the strain of selfishness, lust, and irreligion. He is losing out in our nation as liquor and gambling eat like cancers into the social body and as men forget God in a mad rush for gold and for power. He is losing out in the area of brotherhood as millions suffer under the cruelty of race prejudice. He is losing out in the church as interfaith relations deteriorate more than at any other time in the lives of those now living. He is losing out in the world as an atheistic ideology captures whole nations and as ministers, priests, and missionaries are imprisoned or exiled or killed.

Laymen are coming to understand that a comfortable and complacent discipleship will not meet the needs of this hour. The new interest of laymen is timely, for it is just as true in our day as it was in Paul's day that we wrestle not against mere "flesh and blood, but against principalities, against powers, against the rulers of the darkness of this world, against spiritual wickedness in high places." This is why we must "put on the *whole* armour of God." For the battle which the church must wage in the years ahead will be a tough battle, requiring laymen and laywomen who are spiritually equipped and who love the church enough to sacrifice for it.

Paul knew full well how frail laymen are and how great was the danger that, because of the inadequacy of lay discipleship, God's children might actually be lost! Paul thought of the gospel as a sacred treasure, and he was worried because "we have this treasure in earthen vessels." The earthen vessels, of course, are the ministers and laymen upon whom alone Christ can depend.

Can we love the church as Paul loved it? Can we, too, love Christ so much that we would be his bond servant? Can we love Christ so much that it would be a pleasure to go to jail for him or be shipwrecked for him? Are we laymen willing to take a fresh look at the quality of our discipleship?

Can we pour ourselves out for the church in such a way as to prove to the world our love for Jesus Christ and his church?

This book is an appeal for such a love.

CHAPTER 2

Our Ministers

"It is no small thing to dwell in monasteries, or even in a congregation, and to live there without complaint, and to persevere faithfully even unto death. . . . Here, therefore, men are tried as gold in a furnace."

—Thomas à Kempis

If there were no other reason for loving the church, we would love it for its ministers.

What explains the nobility of the minister's status? Why does the whole community look up to him? Why do the people of his church have a special affection for him?

In the first place, laymen and laywomen admire their minister because he has dedicated his whole life to the service of Jesus Christ. The average consecrated layman is often disturbed by the fact that he can devote only a small part of his time to the service of his Lord.[1] Most of the time of the average layman is spent in making money, and the church gets only his marginal time. But the minister serves Jesus Christ every hour of every day, and because he does so, his laymen naturally look up to him and respect him. His is an honorable and honored calling because of his decision to dedicate his whole life to the service of Christ and his fellow men. Be he ever so modest a person, the minister is set apart and exalted by the very nature of his calling.

In the second place, the people look up to their minister because he is their spiritual leader. Every community has its secular leaders—mayor, councilmen, president of Rotary Club, business executives, school principals, etc.—but not one of these positions can be as lofty as that of the minister, because only he specializes in spiritual leadership. People know full well that our sick world cannot be cured by business or by politics, or even by education, and that it can be cured only by living closer to God. The minister is revered because he specializes in the only kind of leadership that can give us happy homes, wholesome communities, and a peaceful world.

In the third place, the pastor is loved and respected for his personal ministry to the members of his congregation and to their families. When

[1] But see the next chapter, wherein it is pointed out that laymen can use their several occupations as instruments for advancing the cause of Christ.

death or illness strikes, the family turns first to the minister, who responds promptly and lovingly. He brings Christ with him to the bedside, and he never leaves without a prayer. The whole atmosphere of the house is changed because the representative of the church has been there. If there is to be a wedding, the minister officiates, and his ministry at the wedding will be doubly precious because he is God's representative in making two loving souls one for life. It is he who baptizes our children. Indeed, the minister is a sort of spiritual godfather to the whole family and to all the families of his church, and as such he is deeply loved.

It is in his intimate meetings with the official boards of his church that the spiritual insight and ministry of the pastor are especially important. In such meetings he is talking with the lay leaders of the church. Not every minister is aware, it is to be feared, of the vital importance of taking advantage of every such meeting with the officers of his church as an opportunity for breathing his own love for Christ and his own deep concern for the church into the hearts and souls of his lay leaders. One night as such a meeting opened with prayer, I peeked at our minister as he prayed. One would have thought that the whole future of civilization depended on that one little meeting. The minister's face was tense as he prayed. There were deep furrows in his brow. So tightly were his fists clenched that his fingernails seemed to bite into the flesh of his palms as he prayed:

> O God, this is no ordinary meeting. We meet here as disciples of Jesus Christ to carry out his will for our church. Let thy Spirit fill this room. Breathe into us, we pray, thy spiritual fire, because we cannot carry out the program of Jesus Christ unless we are set on fire by the spirit of our Lord. Grant that we may take this meeting very seriously, each one of us, because we meet here as disciples of Jesus Christ and because we need thy guidance in planning for the progress of his church.

How could any meeting of church officers fail to bear fruit when opened with that kind of prayer and conducted in that sort of spiritual atmosphere?

Spiritual fire is like any other fire—it will spread. I have seen it spread from ministers to church officers and from church officers to a great congregation. Laymen must realize, as most ministers realize, the vital importance of developing within their own souls a spiritual warmth and a zeal for Christ so real and so potent that the members of the church will feel it and, feeling it, will share in it.

It is our beloved ministers upon whom we laymen must rely to breathe spiritual fire into us. Only spiritual leadership can save our torn and stricken world. Armies may fight, but, no matter how much they fight, they cannot make the world spiritually right; and no amount of military victories will create the right kind of civilization if people lack spiritual quality. Indeed, the very fact that we are using military methods to solve the world's problems is in itself proof that our Christian civilization has not made sufficient progress. Nor can the desired result be accomplished by legislation. The lawmakers may turn out laws day and night, but legislation cannot save our world. This explains why our ministers are more important than generals, more important than legislators. The world can be saved only by building the right kind of homes and by bringing Christ into the hearts of people everywhere. Gunfire will not end Communism, nor will legislation stop the selfish scramble among nations for the vital commodities of the world. The crying need of this day is for a *faith* that will build a fellowship of men and women throughout the world, a fellowship knit together by devotion to Christ and pledged to bring to all men his love and his peace. To the blessed task of building such a fellowship the minister has devoted his life.

A Passion for Christ

On several occasions ministers have asked me, "What quality is it that a layman most wants in his minister?" That question is rather easy to answer. The layman wants to see in his minister the same quality that the minister wants to see in the layman—a real passion for Christ and a deep love for the church. I have met many ministers and laymen in whose very handclasp I could feel a deep concern for the cause and a willingness to give of self without limit for it. This deep concern, motivated by a great love, is what marks a disciple.

If love for Christ is what it should be, it produces in the disciple, whether minister or layman, a spirit of *restlessness,* a vital concern for the cause, an eternal dissatisfaction with one's efforts for Christ, a constant drive to help to build a better self and a better world, and an increasing willingness to sacrifice for the greatest cause known to man. Such a righteous concern, if general, would end the complacency which is the greatest threat to the church and to the great cause for which the church stands.

Delegation of Responsibility

It is shocking to see the extent to which the average minister feels a responsibility for running the whole church. The more successful a business corporation, the less actual work is done by its president. The president of a successful corporation realizes that he should not do much more than *think and plan,* and he knows that his success will depend on his ability to pick competent men to be responsible for the different phases of the corporation's activities. The success of the average corporation president lies in *delegation of authority and responsibility.*

On the other hand, the average minister, because he feels that the whole burden of the church and its work rests on his shoulders, and because he does not sufficiently challenge his laymen, is frequently engulfed by his work. His average day involves so many duties and responsibilities that he is often both tired and discouraged when evening comes. There are weddings and funerals, infant baptisms, sick calls, committee meetings, conferences of various kinds, ministry to persons in need, and always in the background a certain amount of worry about church finances and about next Sunday's sermon, which he cannot find time to prepare.

Nothing is more important in the life of any minister than the saving of sufficient time for reading and recreation. The minister is a spiritual leader, not an errand boy. The success of the church will depend to a large extent, as does the success of any corporation, on maintaining a right perspective, on skill in planning, and on wise delegation of authority.

Ministers are hurting the church when they work so hard that insufficient time remains for the most important part of a minister's task—developing an adequate program for the church and giving the church a right spiritual tone and direction. A man who is overburdened with tasks and cumbered with too much serving simply cannot give the church the spiritual leadership that it requires.

What It Takes to Be a Minister

The job of being a minister of Jesus Christ is not an easy one. What other calling demands so much selflessness, so much poise, so much grace, so much loyalty, so much love?

How we laymen should pray for our ministers, that God may give them strength and power! How loyally we should support them as they try faithfully to carry on in the name of Jesus Christ! And how clearly we should let them know that, as disciples, we are partners with them in working in the most important cause known to our civilization. Laymen are aware that their own complacency and their lack of zeal make the task of the minister more difficult. Yet one of the duties of a minister is to build around himself a body of eager disciples. This requires not only unlimited patience on the part of the minister, but also much prayer. Often have cold and indifferent church people been changed into warm and zealous disciples by the fervor, the spiritual warmth, and the patience of a minister. Christ converted ordinary workmen into loving disciples. Men are not *born* good church members; they are *made* good church members by someone's patient evangelism.

The lot of the minister is all the harder because of the smallness and meanness of some church people. One would think that church members would have big souls, but some of them have very small souls. At the age of ten I had a glimpse of the smallness of some church women when I visited my grandfather and grandmother in northern New York, where Grandfather was a minister. They lived almost in poverty, because his salary was only $900 per year, not always paid, and they would have starved if it had not been the custom of some of the church members to bring in food to the parsonage. One day the only well-to-do lady in the congregation gave Grandmother a lovely velvet dress trimmed with lace. Grandmother was slender and graceful, with a background of culture and a natural elegance, and she looked stunning in the new dress. She feared to wear it to church, lest it cause criticism, but she did muster up the courage to wear it to a party given by the mayor. Some of the good church ladies were there, too, and several of them criticized Grandmother for wearing such an expensive dress. It so hurt her feelings that she put the lovely garment away and never wore it again.

A word about the importance of ministers' wives and the service they render is in order, because they are not usually given the credit they deserve. If there is any job in this world that is tougher or more blessed than being the wife of a minister, I know not what it is. She must have all the qualities of a saint, and more. She must be a good wife, an ideal mother, a perfect housewife, a clever seamstress, a good teacher, a skilled hostess, a trained diplomat, an expert in psychology, a disciple of Christ. In addition she must give constant moral support to her husband, who, from the very nature of his difficult task, is sure to have periods of discouragement and who will constantly look to her for help and for love. She must supervise many of the activities of the church. She must be expert in pouring Christian oil on troubled waters. She must have the tact of an angel, and withal she must be quite impervious to criticism. I hope that a special place will be reserved in heaven for the wives of our ministers and that special crosses for distinguished service may be awarded them.

The Sermon

We love the church for its sermons. Not all of them are par excellence, but it is seldom that a sermon does not draw us closer to God.

Several ministers have asked what type of sermon laymen like best. That is a very difficult question, but it is certain that the average layman wants a sermon which is based on the Bible, which stresses the basic teachings of Jesus, and which challenges the layman to more adequate Christian living.

Too many sermons are aimed at *comforting* the flock instead of *challenging* the people to more effective discipleship. Ministers must occasionally preach sermons which bring comfort to the distressed, but the average adult church member should have reached the point in his spiritual development where he is thinking in terms of manifesting Christ to other people, instead of looking for solace himself. Not enough sermons challenge church members to Christian evangelism and to heroic Christian service. As the Rev. Maldwyn A. Davies says, "The sermon must agitate or disturb; it must impel the mind of the listener to a verdict. If the congregation merely 'likes' or 'enjoys' the sermon, it has missed its mark." It is not enough in this day to have sermons which are skillfully arranged and impressively delivered, or which merely delight the audience. What the world needs and must have is laymen who manifest a love for Jesus Christ, and who have the courage to bring his love and his saving grace to suffering humanity. Dr. Walter Barlow's indictment of Protestant preaching is very serious if true: "The sorrowful fact must be admitted that the Protestantism of the first half of this century has seen the evangelistic note die down to a whisper in vast numbers of pulpits, while in some that same note has been deliberately silenced." [2]

I recently asked a very able minister why so many sermons seem to lack evangelistic zeal. He made an unexpected reply: "We have on our seminary faculties too many intellectuals, many of whom lack real zeal for Christ." Next, I asked him to explain the lack of zeal among laymen. He replied: "If there is not zeal in the pulpit, there will not be zeal in the pews."

What Is the Aim of the Sermon?

Ministers should never preach a sermon which does not reveal their own deep love for Christ. If I were a minister, I believe that I would apply one or more of the following tests to each of my own sermons:

[2] *God So Loved* (Westwood, N. J.: Fleming H. Revell Co., 1952), p. 13.

Will this sermon burn into the hearts of my people the deep and eternal significance of Jesus Christ and the world's need for him?

Will this sermon make my people appreciate the great miracle of life, the precious value of each hour, and the possibility of laying hold of the abundant life by conforming to the laws of God?

Will this sermon inspire my people to pray and to pray earnestly?

Will this sermon make my people love the Bible and want to read it?

Will this sermon help in the building of better homes and a better community?

Will this sermon reveal my own love for Jesus Christ and for his church?

Will this sermon point out to my laymen what it means to be a disciple of Jesus Christ and challenge them to more adequate Christian living?

Will this sermon convince my hearers that the world situation is serious, and that some of the most precious things in our Christian culture are being lost?

Will this sermon make my people feel that they are Christ's minutemen, who alone can save the world from destruction?

Will this sermon warn my people that the plans and the lives of men will fail unless God is in them?

Will this sermon impress upon my people the fact that the church is putting up a hard fight on many a battlefront across the world and that often there is danger of losing the battle because of inadequate lay support?

Will this sermon give my people a vision of a world-wide brotherhood of disciples of Jesus Christ, consisting of many millions of Christian people, who are working together to establish the kingdom of God on earth?

Will this sermon make my laymen and laywomen want to use their businesses and their professions as instruments for advancing the cause of Christ?

Will this sermon make my laymen and laywomen feel that they are the church and that as such they must manifest Jesus Christ in all their daily work and contacts?

Most important of all, will this sermon make my people more conscious of God and draw them closer to him?

Ministers have complained that even when they preach with the utmost vigor, the response of laymen is often so slight as to be discouraging. One day in a moment of discouragement the late Peter Marshall said to me, "I preach and I preach and I preach *and nothing happens.*"

Said I in reply, "How dare you say, Peter, that nothing happens? The gospel of Jesus Christ is so valid and the principles set forth in the Bible are so eternally sound that it is impossible to preach the gospel without something happening. The result may not be visible immediately, but an impression is made on the hearts of the people." I then cited an instance in my own life when, facing a crisis, I was helped by a sermon preached *twenty years before.*

The impression made on the hearers will depend in part on the fidelity with which the minister adheres to the gospel and in part on his success in making his hearers share his concern and his love.

CHAPTER 3

The Christian Layman

"The great heresy of this day is not lack of faith in God but lack of faith in the power of our laymen."

—John Charles McKirachan

We love the church for its laymen.

All over this nation I have met them—businessmen, lawyers, bankers, physicians, teachers, labor leaders, farmers, workmen, judges, scientists—a fine cross section of the best in American life, and of the caliber that can help America lead the world out of its present chaos.

But in spite of the quality of our laymen it is appalling to think of the terrific job that Christian laymen, in co-operation with their ministers, have before them. Being a Christian layman these days is no sinecure. A lost world must be saved, and it cannot be saved by ministers alone.

We Are the Church

We laymen have fallen into the habit of thinking of the church as a sanctuary, plus a minister, plus a choir, plus a Sunday school. *The truth is that we laymen with our ministers are the church.* We have, of course, a sanctuary in which we meet together for worship under the inspired leadership of our minister, a choir to facilitate our worship, and a Sunday school for the Christian education of our children; but all these are only aids to help us. *We are the church.*

But it is not only when we worship that we constitute the church. We are just as much a part of the church when we are behind the plow or sitting at our office desk as when we occupy the pews. Indeed it is not in the pew that we render our best service for Jesus Christ, but at our workbench, wherever it may be. The true church consists of a group of consecrated laymen, at work for Christ in the world, manifesting Christ at home with their families and in their various business, social, and civic relationships.

This business of being a disciple of Jesus Christ is serious business, and it is necessary that we laymen ask ourselves every day of the week, "What more can I do for Christ than I am now doing?" This old world of ours will be won for Christ only if we laymen regard our work for the church as the most important work we do in life, and prove it by exerting ourselves to the utmost. Oswald Chambers' book *My Utmost for His Highest* will be found most helpful to any layman who wants to take Christ more seriously.[1]

Laymen constitute the only "bridge" over which Jesus Christ can move from the church into the community. We sometimes forget that it is not in the church that Christ is most needed, but in the business world and along the highways and byways of life. The minister has no opportunity to carry Christ into the courtroom, the business office, the plant, the factory, or the bank. If Christ is to be carried into these places, we laymen must take him there.

Often we laymen make the mistake of thinking of a church as an end to be served rather than as Jesus' means to an end. It is a mistake to think of serving the church for the *purpose* of serving the church. Without minimizing in the least the importance of the work that laymen do for the church, for it is vitally important work, we must remember that the church sanctuary is in reality a spiritual service station to which we laymen go on Sunday for the purpose of getting our spiritual batteries recharged for work *in the community during the balance of the week.* We look to Christ to use the minister and the worship service to charge our low spiritual batteries.

A Layman's Faith

I must be utterly frank and truthful about my own experience with God. I would be neither if I should claim that I always had faith in God. There were times, especially in my earlier years, when I had grave doubts about God and about religion in general. And I must confess that even in these later years there have been times when I was forced to say, "Lord, I believe; help thou mine unbelief."

Sometimes I wonder whether a man can have a strong faith without having passed through periods of doubt. The successful businessman is the one who has fought his way through many hardships. The successful marriage is the one in which the partners have prayed their way through many differences, often serious, and often accompanied by copious tears. The man of strong character is the man who has lost one moral battle after another but who, with the help of prayer, has finally won. The good old Latin motto *Per aspera ad astra* (Through hardships to the stars) is as valid today as it ever was.

It is so with faith. We are not born with a strong faith, nor is it handed to any man on a silver platter. We acquire a strong faith by

[1] 4th ed.; New York: Dodd, Mead & Co., 1952.

fighting our way through difficulties and doubts. Faith is the result of many battles within one's soul. Often in my own experience I have gained two steps toward God only to lose three steps.

Faith often requires waiting for God. His timing is often far different from our timing. We are very impatient; he is not. Our planning is human; his planning is divine. The average layman finds that salvation comes gradually, and often after a real struggle with self. As Paul Moser so beautifully points out, Jesus is *continuously* at work within us, trying to bring us to God. He stands at the door and knocks, not once, but all the time, trying to penetrate our hard and selfish hearts.

It is unreasonable to expect real faith to develop if we will not work at it. It is impossible to experience God if we will not give him a chance in our lives. He cannot enter closed hearts. But it is an invariable rule that he will enter the open heart.

Without God, life for me would lose its purpose and its direction. Indeed, I see no reason for living if I am but the fortuitous result of the accidental behavior of atoms in a cosmic test tube. Life is rich and precious because it fits into a divine plan and harmonizes with all else in this wonderful universe to the extent that I obey the laws of God and try to follow in the footsteps of Jesus Christ.

What we self-centered and comfortable laymen need more than anything else is to stop loving ourselves and to fall in love with Jesus Christ. When we do that, we begin to love other people, and we begin to catch something of the significance of the cross. The cross emancipates us by freeing us from self-worship and by making us the servants of humanity. We are thus transformed from laymen with a big ego to laymen who say devotedly, "Here I am, Lord; use me." May God burn into our hearts and souls the high meaning of the cross. It requires a great faith and a real courage to transform a fellow from a self-serving, ego-centered individual into a loving and expendable disciple of Jesus Christ. But it is only men who are thus transformed who can love the world into brotherhood and peace.

American Laymen

It may be appropriate at this time to refer to a few strong laymen who have built successful lives through a combination of consecration and courage.

Harold R. Medina. When things got tough during the Communists' trial, Judge Medina would retire to his private chambers to pray to God for strength to carry on for the sake of America, for the sake of democracy, and for the sake of our fine judicial system.

Walter Judd. This former medical missionary to China, now Congressman from Minnesota, has such a real concern for the gospel of Christ that he literally wears himself out making speeches and otherwise spending his energy for the cause of Christ. He sees the danger of immorality in high places and the desperate need of millions throughout the world.

Luther W. Youngdahl. Judge of the United States District Court for the District of Columbia, where he now participates extensively in religious activities, this Christian layman was selected "Outstanding Layman for the Year 1949" by the Federated Lutheran Clubs of our nation.

Charles E. Wilson. Starting his career in a smelly factory which manufactured electric-conduit fittings, he rose to be head of General Electric Company and to be appointed Director of the Office of Defense Mobilization. The secret of his success is found partly in the fact that he was born into a truly Christian home—located ironically enough in New York's crime-ridden "Hell's Kitchen."

James Lewis Kraft.[2] There is no greater romance in American industry than the rise of this layman from farm boy to the world's largest cheese manufacturer. And a glorious feature of his meteoric rise is that he gave God all the credit for it. Probably to a greater extent than any other man he backed the International Council of Religious Education.

Arthur S. Flemming. When the military situation in Korea made it urgently necessary to mobilize the nation's entire manpower, he was selected for the job under Charles E. Wilson, Director of the Office of Defense Mobilization. Arthur Flemming was the first layman to be president of Ohio Wesleyan University, "Mother of Bishops."

What It Takes to Be a Good Layman

Laymen are constantly asking, "What are the tests of a good church member?" The following are suggested:

1. Character. It is impossible to get in tune with God if there is something in our life that our conscience tells us is wrong. It is the pure in heart who see God. Conscience is the wonderful guide which God has given us to tell us whether we are doing right or wrong. We must use our will power in the God-direction indicated by conscience and by the teachings of our Master. Says Rabbi Silver: "A man of

[2] Mr. Kraft passed away after this was written, but his spirit still lives.

character begins his program for the rebuilding of society with himself."

2. A strong faith. The good layman lives confidently because of his faith in God and in Jesus Christ. The successful layman takes every situation in stride because of the assurance that everything is part of a divine plan, and because he always trusts his Creator.

3. Loyalty to Jesus Christ. A sensitiveness to Jesus Christ requires constant effort and constant checking. Men do not lose their Christianity because someone has argued them away from it. Men lose their Christianity through just plain carelessness and just plain laziness in the use of their minds and of their will power. If we are to preserve our faith, we must keep working everlastingly at it, just as an athlete must faithfully practice if he is to keep himself fit. We all feel loyal to our Lord while we are in church. But the real test comes in the market place, in the athletic contest, and in the midst of the daily temptations and pressures of life.

4. Sensitiveness to the things of God. Why does one man hate and fear race prejudice while another considers it more or less natural and proper? Why does one man shudder at the awful carnage at Hiroshima while another laughs it off as "something the rascals deserved"? Why does one man go faithfully to church, even in bad weather, while another stays home and reads the sports page? Why does one man pray for the success of the United Nations while another hopes we shall blow all the Communists into eternity with the atomic bomb, and the sooner the better? These questions suggest that men differ as to their sensitiveness to the higher things. There is no way to acquire a fine sensitiveness except by earnest study of the example of One who willingly gave his life that men might be sensitively attuned to the heart of God.

5. Gratitude to God. The devoted follower of Jesus Christ has in his heart at all times a feeling of deep gratitude for life, for God, and for Jesus Christ. Such a person constantly says to himself: "How wonderful to be alive! What a privilege to be a child of God! How blessed to be a member of the Church of Jesus Christ!" The disciple lives as if he were part of a great miracle, as indeed he is.

6. Faithful stewardship. The good church member feels that he holds in trust something very precious. His life and his property do not belong to him, but to God. His attitude is one of ready willingness: "What wilt thou have me to do?" He serves because he loves.

7. Hard work. God wants his children to be fruitful. He despises the sluggard, but he loves the builder. The good layman places such high value on life and on the importance of the church that he tries not to waste a minute, but is every day and every hour a faithful servant of his Lord.

8. Prayer. One cannot be a faithful follower of Jesus Christ without earnest prayer. Prayer keeps us tuned up. Prayer gives a right direction to life. Prayer helps to get out of our lives the things that separate us from God. There is nothing to equal prayer as a power for the building of the good life.

9. Companionship with God. The real disciple has a constant feeling of the omnipresence of God. The presence of God is very real to him in his home, in his office, in all his contacts with other people. To have this feeling of God's omnipresence gives a person a daily confidence and a faith that enable him to carry on, even under difficulties.

10. A feeling of expendability. It is quite possible to love Christ so much that we will work for him even when we are too tired to work. It is possible to love him so much that we will give money to the church even when by so doing we are deprived of something we want for ourselves. It is possible to love Christ so much that we will take a church-committee chairmanship even if we are already overburdened with other work. The good layman repeatedly says to himself, "I am not living this life for my own enjoyment but to honor God." The good layman is as expendable as the soldier in battle.

11. A great love. "But the greatest of these is love." In the area of Christian discipleship there is no substitute for love. The best disciple is the one who is most in love with his Lord. Thomas à Kempis prayed that he might love God in the same way that a lover adores his sweetheart. Jesus wants disciples who are in love with God and with his church.

United Church Men

We love the church because it inspires a burning desire for unity among the disciples of Christ, whatever their sign or seal. There is in the hearts of laymen, perhaps even more than in the hearts of ministers, a great eagerness to overcome the things that divide and to find ways of working together more effectively.

The establishment of the National Council of the Churches of Christ in America, representing thirty communions, has been one of the most encouraging signs of a new-found ability to unify efforts. Happily, too, the National Council has had the vision to see the importance of laymen's work. At its constituting convention in Cleveland in 1950 the blueprints of a general department of United Church Men were drafted.

In October of 1951 the United Church Men of America was publicly inaugurated with Lem T. Jones, a consecrated manufacturer of Kansas City, Missouri, as chairman of the board of managers and E. Urner Goodman, for many years National Program Director of the Boy Scouts of America, as general director.

The members of United Church Men conceive of themselves as crusaders whose purpose it is to bring together in Christian fellowship and action the men of the thirty member denominations in order to give practical expression to their allegiance to their Lord and Saviour, Jesus Christ.

United Church Men specializes in inspiring the individual layman to a more deeply consecrated discipleship. The leaders of the movement at the national level are themselves outstanding Christian laymen, and men of long experience in lay activity. They know that the men's work in the church can be successful only to the extent that *every man of the church is reached, and his interest kept alive.*

Elton Trueblood says that "if in the average church we should suddenly take seriously the notion that every lay member, man or woman, is really a minister of Christ, we could have something like a revolution in a very short time." [3]

Probably the most interesting and inspiring project which the National Council is now pushing through its new department, United Church Men, is what is called the Every Man Plan. Under this plan the entire membership of the local church is enlisted for service. By dividing the men of the local church into small groups of five men each, the foundation is laid for a campaign the object of which is to get every man in his pew on Sunday and to integrate every man into the work and the life of the church.[4]

Onward, Christian Soldiers

There is one further note to be added to this story of united discipleship. In May of 1952 leaders of men's work from nine European countries, together with the general director of the United Church Men of America, met together at the Ecumenical Institute in Switzerland, under the auspices of the World Council of Churches, to plan a world strategy and again to share their successful experiences.

This coming together of church people throughout the free lands of the world seems like a direct response to the prayer of Jesus "that they

[3] *Your Other Vocation* (New York: Harper & Bros., 1952), p. 29.

[4] Detailed information may be obtained from the Department of United Church Men, National Council of Churches, 257 Fourth Avenue, New York 10, New York.

all may be one; . . . that the world may believe that thou hast sent me."

We American laymen are not alone in this great task. It is reliably stated that in Europe alone there are over thirteen million of the Reformed faith. The biggest job confronting the church today at the international level is to strengthen the ties that bind together these millions of followers of Jesus Christ. That is why the work of our boards of foreign missions must be given high priority. It is their missionaries, their schools and hospitals, their mission stations, that are doing so much to create a Christian atmosphere in many lands.

There is no organization in this whole world other than the Church of Jesus Christ which can weld men into a united brotherhood on both sides of the Iron Curtain. Indeed the Church defies the Iron Curtain as millions of laymen on both sides of it lift their voices in prayer to God for freedom and for world peace. The existence of this world-wide brotherhood in Christ is the one challenge which Communism is unable to meet, and which it will never meet.

CHAPTER 4

The Miracle of Life

"The most important fact in life is that creative and sustaining unity which we call God."

—Eugene Exman

It was the church that gave me a right understanding of life and opened my eyes to the wonder and the beauty of God's universe.

Of all God's miracles, by far the greatest is the human life. How wonderful is the little span of years which an infinite Sculptor has carved out of his eternity for us! All of life is a miracle, and each day is filled with miracles, large and small. Even a drop of water is a miracle, consisting as it does of two gases combined for our benefit. The air is a miracle; our ability to breathe it is a miracle; how the breathing of it enables us to live is a miracle.

As a boy I often lay on my back on the grass on a starry night and studied the heavens. To this day the moon impresses me as a miracle, suspended in the sky as it is, just far enough from the earth to provide us with the soft beauty of reflected light. The sun is another miracle, flung into infinite space just far enough from the earth to give us the right degree of warmth. Even to this day I have a feeling of awe when I realize that our earth and we human beings are being catapulted through space at more than two hundred times the speed of a fast passenger plane, yet the water on the face of a lake is so beautifully calm and undisturbed that one can see trees mirrored in it. How, I have asked myself for many years, can everything be so calm and so peaceful about us if our world is speeding through the universe at nearly 67,000 miles an hour?

The stars have always intrigued me. It was at the very time in my boyhood when I was studying the heavens so earnestly that my Sunday-school teacher asked me to memorize the eighth psalm, which contains these words: "When I consider thy heavens, the work of thy fingers, the moon and the stars, which thou hast ordained; what is man, that thou art mindful of him? and the son of man, that thou visitest him?"

Even in my early years I was poignantly aware of the smallness of man and the greatness of God's universe. In mathematics class I was intrigued by what seemed to me to be the relationship between mathematics and the laws of the universe. So systematic is the movement of the stars that by the use of mathematics men accurately determine the position which a star will occupy years hence. But what intrigued me most was the concept of *infinity*. Even before I studied mathematics, I was captivated by what seemed to me a universe without any beginning or any end. And when later I came across that wonderful observation by Tagore, the poet of India, that "there is comfort in the contemplation of Infinity," I had no difficulty in grasping the deep significance of it, for already as a lad I had begun to feel my absolute dependence on an infinite Creator, whose handiwork was not only evident to me on every hand but obviously so marvelous as to be beyond human comprehension.

There are other miracles just as great as the heavens. Within the tiny atom we find other astounding miracles. In fact, one of God's greatest miracles is the atom. So small that it would take 120,000 hydrogen atoms, for example, laid side by side, to equal the width of a human hair, these atoms contain within themselves enough latent energy to destroy a whole city!

The miracles outside the world of physical science have always seemed to me to be even more wonderful and certainly more beautiful than those in the realm of physics. I refer, for example, to the song of a bird, to a mother's love, to the inexpressible beauty of the flowers, to the perfect formation of an orange, to the laughter of a child.

We are reminded by E. Urner Goodman that we laymen are prone to think of too little a God, and that the true God "must be a God of all the Universe, while at the same time he is heavenly Father to each of us, for his infinity stretches outward in endless space and inward to the heart of the least of us mortals." The modern layman has no difficulty in agreeing that the only God that can satisfy the human soul is one much larger than the capacity of our human minds to understand. Says Professor W. O. Doescher: "Whoever would persuade the enlightened mind today, however, must preach a God worthy of the sublime Being revealed in nature, from the atom to the spiral nebulae." [1]

When Henry Norris Russell, Princeton astronomer, had concluded a lecture on the Milky Way, a woman came to him and said, "If our world is so little and the universe is so great, can we really believe that God pays any attention to us?"

[1] "Natural Science and Christian Theology," *Theology Today*, IX (October, 1952), No. 3, 314.

Dr. Russell replied, "That, Madam, depends entirely on how big a God you believe in."

Shall We Doubt the Miracles?

I always smile when men raise a question about belief in God. I smile because the air they breathe came from God. The force of gravity which enables them to walk on the earth came from God. The sunlight which grows their food came from God. The water they drink came from God. Their very bodies came from God. And even the minds with which they doubt him came fom God! Yes, I smile when I see these God-made creatures living in a God-made environment arguing as to whether they should believe in God! As Harold A. Bosley so beautifully puts it, all life is dealing with God, whether consciously or not. We have no option, says Bosley, as to whether we shall live with God; our option relates only to *how* we shall live with him.[2] And shall we exercise the option by denying his existence and by failing even to admit the reality of his marvelous laws which make it possible for us to breathe, and see and work and love?

During a brief period of time—terribly brief when measured against God's infinity—we are permitted to walk on this marvelous little planet, and breathe, and taste, and love, and build, and dream, and, what is most wonderful of all, perfect our human selves by getting our hearts and minds more and more in tune with the heart and the mind of our divine Creator.

This possibility of spiritual growth is one of the greatest of all miracles. It is due to another miracle—a little bit of God which he has placed in each one of us and which we call "Soul." In the whole realm of the natural and the supernatural what can be more miraculous than to find a part of the divine spirit within our human bodies? What greater miracle than the soul, by the growth of which we can increase our spiritual stature so as to lift ourselves above the difficulties and the trials of the material world and live victoriously and triumphantly as children of God?

The fact that this human life of ours is the greatest of all God's miracles casts a heavy responsibility upon us to live each day at our best, to have constantly in mind the highest goals we know, to be always aware of the miracle of life and of the countless miracles, large and small, with which each day is filled. We love the church because of its emphasis upon the miraculous nature of this human life, and

[2] *On Final Ground* (New York: Harper & Bros., 1946), p. 3.

because it keeps constantly before our eyes the figure of Jesus Christ, whom God sent to us to remind us of his divine love for us and to urge us to live, not as worried and defeated humans, but confidently, fearlessly, and victoriously, as children of a truly infinite God.

It grieves me to see so many men plod through life without catching anything of its loveliness or its beauty. I think of the colorless, materialistic world described by Herman Hagedorn, who pictures men as

> Prisoners in this world of coins and wires and motor horns,
> This world of figures and of men who trust in facts,
> This pitiable, hypocritic world where men with blinkered
> eyes and hobbled feet
> Grope down a narrow gorge and call it life![3]

The very first and most essential step in religion is to cultivate an appreciation of our God-given life and to love and worship the Giver. We love the church because it specializes in training people to know and to love God and because it constantly holds before our eyes Jesus Christ as the Way of life.

As one's appreciation of the miracle of life grows, he automatically draws nearer to God. He begins to see and feel God in everything. He comes to understand what Oswald Chambers means when he says that God "engineers our circumstances," and what Muriel Lester means when she speaks of "practicing the presence of God."

The fact that we are human, while God is infinite, means necessarily that we shall never completely understand him. Perhaps it is fortunate that the whole truth is always beyond our reach. There is something beautiful and inspiring about a human mind that is forever reaching out toward an infinite God. Harry A. Overstreet says: "The mind that keeps the pathways of truth open is humble before possibilities not yet disclosed."

When I see men like the inspired writer of the Psalms and my own pastor drawn closer to God by the majesty of the mountains, and when I hear the psalmist proclaim that "the heavens declare the glory of God; and the firmament sheweth his handywork," and when I find myself standing humble and in awe before the unspeakable beauty of snow-capped Jungfrau resplendent in the moonlight, it becomes easy to agree with Paul Althaus that "nature prevents one from being an atheist."

[3] From "The Great Maze" and "The Heart of Youth" (New York: The Macmillan Co., 1916). Used by permission.

At such times one can readily believe with Professor Doescher that "Christian culture alone inspired men to approach the study of nature with devotion and with the eager confidence that she would reward her devotees with a vision of divine wisdom and glory." [4]

Why does the Christian look upon all of life as a miracle? Because to the Christian God is in everything—in every act, in every friendship, in every atom, in every song, in every thought. When once we get this feeling of "God in everything," life indeed becomes a miracle, and every hour precious.

[4] *Op. cit.*, p. 309.

CHAPTER 5

The Abundant Life

"I am come that they might have life, and that they might have it more abundantly."

—John 10:10

Everyone craves fullness of life. A real man wants to live life to the full, to be productive, to count for something. Men of caliber are even willing to live dangerously if they think that dangerous living will help in the building of a better world. We love the church because it specializes in bringing the abundant life to all.

The average layman of today insists upon a religion that *really works* when applied to life. The great value of the Christian religion is that *it works*. The trouble with us laymen is that we don't give it a chance. When a great Britisher was asked how the Christian religion was getting along in England, he replied, "I don't know—it's never been tried!" Nor has it ever been really tried in any nation. But to the extent that we do apply it we find that it makes happy homes, it gives children a right attitude toward life, it brings peace of mind, it gives purpose and perspective to life, it encourages peace instead of war, it makes for righteousness in a community.

I am unable to see how life can be purposeful or abundant apart from God. Certainly I am incapable of creating, aside from God, a pattern into which my life will fit so as to make it meaningful. But as soon as I bring God into the picture, my little span of years becomes part of a tremendous pattern, capable of being used as an instrument for the building of a better world, for lifting burdens from the hearts of other people, for bringing hope to those in despair, for protecting the dignity and the sanctity of man, for fighting the wrong in my local community, for helping to lift my nation above the plane of selfish nationalism, for taking a stand against those who would make government the master of its people, for playing my small part in the building of a brotherhood of men under God. Jesus has shown so clearly and beautifully how an ordinary human existence can be transformed into a glowing, purposeful life and how it can be made to fit into a divine plan.

The average man is a builder. He wants to till the soil, or build bridges, or write a book, or minister to people, or teach youth, or heal the sick. Men want to be creative. Almost instinctively they feel that God wants them to help in the building of something, as indeed he does. For God himself is a Builder, and he expects us to help him build. We love the church because it is ever stressing the laws of God. By following these laws men can build a happy, fruitful life, and make this little human span a part of something much greater—something that has its origin and its fulfillment in eternity.

There can be no failure in such a life, and no despair. Hardships and even ill health may come, but they will be borne unflinchingly, as God can readily convert ill into good. Tragedy may come (Christ was led to his death), but even tragedy may be converted into triumph, as it was on the cross.

The richness of life is due mainly to the spiritual forces within and about us. The courage that enables a man to stand firm against adversity; the hope that rises above defeat; the sacrificial spirit that makes parents willing to suffer anything for their children; the beauty of friendship; mercy that extends a helping hand; compassion that enables one to suffer with and for another—these are among the values that make life worth while. But above all is the saving power of Jesus Christ, which even today lifts men from the gutter, even today mends broken homes, even today transforms men from prosaic, weak human creatures into confident, radiant disciples.

Serenity of Soul

We love the church because it helps its members to achieve serenity of soul. People talk about happiness as the great objective, but true serenity is a higher goal—the blessed state where all trouble has disappeared or has been overcome by faith, all subconscious complexes brought out into the light and mastered, all hatreds and jealousies ejected, all lusts and passions brought under perfect control, all worry banished. When this is accomplished, the soul is as calm and serene as the placid water of a lake on a quiet summer evening.

If only we could understand that Jesus came to lift us to a higher plane of living—to enable us, through the grace of God, to live as men should live who are the children of infinite power and infinite love! One wonders why we persist in being the victims of fear and trouble when there is available to us, if we will but use it, an unlimited reservoir of spiritual power.

Georgia Harkness, one of the great disciples of Christ in our day, has discovered the real secret of the serene life. This inspired Christian leader writes: "A large part of the Christian life is a quest for the peace of mind that comes from having an ultimate ground of confidence, and this to the Christian means having one's soul stayed upon God." [1]

The Speed and Pressure of Modern Living

A practical difficulty confronting all of us is the speed of our modern living. There seems to be something about the tempo of our lives that scarcely leaves time for appreciation of the beautiful. When our minister, Dr. Hollister, returned recently from an auto trip, he preached an inspiring sermon entitled "The New Jersey Turnpike." He pictured dramatically the high speeds which so effectively swallow up distance that they almost bring New York Harbor and Delaware Bay together. But, Dr. Hollister continued:

> We suddenly realized that something was wrong. There was no beauty. We were tense. We had even lost our individuality because everybody was traveling at sixty miles per hour. So we turned aside into a country road where we could smell the breath of new-mown hay, and see the trees hanging heavy with fruit, and even stop to chat with a farmer. We became human again.

Much of our restlessness is due to our concern about the future. Today's happiness is stunted by our subconscious fear as to what the morrow may bring. If only we had the capacity to live abundantly today, to breathe today's glorious air, to marvel in today's glorious sunshine, to wonder at the beauty of today's flowers, to treasure today's love, to feel God's nearness today!

Serenity of soul is not easily attained in our world. It is acquired only by putting up a fight against the influences, not inappropriately called "the wiles of the devil," which are a constant threat to the abundant life. The appeal of sex, the thirst for liquor, the attractive seductions that cause disloyalty, the ease and comfort of selfish living, the nice feeling of superiority that accompanies race prejudice, the love of money, the pride of position—all these stand in the way of the abundant life which our Lord wants all of us to have.

If we have Christ in our hearts, we shall live in such a manner that the abundant life which we have attained will spread to others. Someone has said that whenever we meet another person, that person is either spiritually worse or spiritually better because he met us. It is a challenging thought that we cannot avoid influencing other people.

[1] *Prayer and the Common Life* (New York and Nashville: Abingdon-Cokesbury Press, 1948), p. 96.

If we desire to live in an atmosphere of gloom and despair, it is quite possible for us to do so. There are some folks who seem actually to take pleasure in being mournful. Their gloom spreads to others. Soon a whole household or office is on the verge of despair because of one small, gloomy soul.

On the other hand, optimism is equally catching. We can, if we wish, be cheerful and buoyant no matter how rough the path. This is not a blind sort of Pollyanna optimism which exudes artificial or synthetic happiness, but rather the kind of quiet faith which enables a heroic soul to smile through his tears.

What a world this would be if every man and woman in it refused to give up, refused to admit defeat, grew strong through discouragement, triumphed over pain! We could bring heaven to earth if we had the necessary faith and courage.

To the sad or lonely soul we should say: "Jesus is waiting for you. His power and his love are at your disposal." "Ask, and ye shall receive."

We love the church because we find within it people who are seeking earnestly to find the abundant life, and who are not afraid to live dangerously in order to provide the abundant life for others. We must avoid the idea that we are seeking a life of ease and comfort for ourselves. The meaning of the Cross is that we should, at whatever cost, seek the abundant life for all God's children.

CHAPTER 6

Aiming at the Stars

"In God alone is to be found the power that through the ages has impelled men to the performance of the highest duty, has inspired them to the most unselfish service, has given them the strength to make the greatest sacrifices."

—John D. Rockefeller, Jr.

We love the church because it keeps our eyes turned toward life's highest goal. The church is constantly and lovingly reminding men that life has a rich meaning and that life's highest values are discovered by those who keep ever before them the highest and best. The church specializes in teaching us how to lift our sights, how to open our eyes and see God.

To me religion represents the sum total of man's response to God's unceasing attempt to reach him. Almost from the dawn of civilization men have been reaching out for a fuller appreciation of God. We see this in philosophy's attempt to discover the purpose and the rationale of life. We see it in poetry's attempt to lift men above themselves. We see it in the loveliness of music as the indescribable beauty of mingled strings and the blending of human voices lift us out of the disharmony of life's daily routine into the glorious symphony of the orchestra and the choir. We see it on the painter's canvas as he translates into beauty the deepest longings of the soul. We see it in the thinking of the skilled psychiatrist as he seeks to untangle the confused thinking of the mentally sick and to point out to the sufferer the mental pain that comes from wrong thinking and uncontrolled emotions and the joyous health and mental peace that come when the mind and heart of man are attuned to the heart and mind of God.

In each of these areas the main effort has been to lift men to a higher plane of living and to reveal to man his unlimited potentialities as a child of God. Religion is simply the systematizing of all these processes of outreach, and religion therefore embraces philosophy, poetry, music, art, psychology, and every other process by which men reach out for God. When the world got badly off the track and men were relying on military strength and on human force and brutality instead of on the principles of God, Jesus came to show, with matchless clarity and with great beauty, how men might through love and faith find their way back to God. And a world spiritually off the track today can be saved by the same Christ if, and only if, ministers and laymen will display a better quality of Christian discipleship.

Spiritual Growth

A loving God created our universe and breathed life into us human beings. He did so because he is building a kingdom. For reasons best known to himself he made *growth* and *responsibility* important factors in the building of the kingdom. He could have made us, if he so wished, so perfect that no growth or responsibility would be necessary. But it is evident, even to our human minds, that it would be a strange sort of world in which no work had to be done because God had arranged for grains and fruits to grow by themselves and because he had provided, for example, millions of perfect automobiles to save us the trouble of manufacturing them. Even with our little minds we can see the value of growth and of responsibility, and the indispensability of work in any process of building.

God must have decided deliberately, therefore, that growth was to be the very basis of his evolving kingdom. He made it possible for us to grow by giving us the power to decide between right and wrong. Quite obviously if we did not have the power to decide to be bad, we could not have the power to decide to be good. A loving God, therefore, gave us the choice, and sent Jesus to us to demonstrate the value and the necessity of a right choice, and the peril in a bad choice.

Jesus tells us that we are workers in God's kingdom; that we must help build the kingdom; that we have a deep responsibility in the matter; that there are certain rules and laws by which we must be guided if we are to build aright, including the Ten Commandments and the principles of the Sermon on the Mount; that if we build aright, we shall find our reward in being accepted as part of God's eternal kingdom, which means that we shall have eternal life. It is just that simple, but it involves heavy responsibility and hard work.

The laws which a loving God has provided for our daily living are no less wonderful than the physical laws which control the movement of the stars and the behavior of the atom. The law that peace is better than war; the law that love is better than hatred; the law that humility is better than pride; the law that sacrifice is better than selfishness; the law that diligence is better than shiftlessness; the law that integrity is better than looseness of character; the law that mercy is better than cruelty—these laws are just as valid, just as important, and just as inexorable as the law of gravity. We love the church because it is forever stressing the laws and principles of God by which, if we are willing, we can live up to the highest and best.

If we violate the physical laws of the universe by descending too steep a precipice, we are almost sure to get hurt. And in the same way, if we forget that humility is better than pride, we shall also get hurt, because even our friends will not love us; and if we forget that integrity is better than dishonesty, we may land in jail. The principles and the laws of God as set forth in the Bible and as exemplified in the life of Jesus Christ are essential to the good life and to true happiness. We violate them at our peril.

The secret of religious living is to make a small soul grow into a big soul. One of the main differences between the consecrated person and the nonreligious person is that the latter gives little if any thought to the development of his soul, being quite content to have a little soul, whereas the consecrated person specializes in increasing the size of his soul. The building of a Christian culture consists mainly of the changing of little souls into big souls by breathing the spirit of Christ into the hearts of men.

I love the story of the little girl whose mother took her to school for the first time. The school was only a short distance from her home, but the mother feared that the child might get lost in returning from school. Near their home was a church with a tall white steeple, so the mother said to the little girl, "When you come out of the school, just look for the white steeple and walk toward it, and you will get home safely."

For the first couple of days everything went well, and the steeple proved to be an unfailing guide. But on the third day the teacher dismissed the class through another door on the opposite side of the building, and there was no steeple to be seen. The little girl began to cry, and one of the teachers came out of the school to find out what the trouble was. "I can't find the steeple," said the little girl.

She was led over to the other side of the school building, where the steeple was plainly evident, and the whole problem was solved.

We all need something to guide us in this life. If we do not have it, there is danger of our becoming lost. We love the church because it provides the "steeple" which prevents us from becoming lost.

General Omar Bradley recently pleaded with our nation to keep high its goals. "We must be guided by the stars and not by the lights of each passing ship," he said. We love the church because it helps us to be "guided by the stars."

CHAPTER 7

Our Precious Heritage

"Democracy is a stern and lofty creed of willing self-denial, of responsibility staunchly borne."

—George Arthur Frantz

We love the church because it safeguards the best in Christian America.

Ours is indeed a precious heritage. I am not one of the hopeless conservatives who resist changes in our social life. Far from it. The gospel of Jesus Christ is a dynamic gospel, and those who really believe in it can never be defenders of the *status quo*. Yet I am persuaded that hidden in the Stars and Stripes are precious values which were put there by the courage and the sacrifice of our forefathers—values which, if we safeguard them, will preserve our freedom and protect the dignity of man as a child of God.

When the colonists came to these shores, they came to find true freedom. Most of them were Christians who brought their Bibles with them. History will show that they never founded a village without building a church. And as they blazed a difficult trail through the wilderness, fighting Indians and enduring unspeakable hardships, they relied on their own muscles and their faith in God, and, incidentally, they received no bonus checks from Washington. There is in our nation today a dangerous trend toward big government and toward fascism, for the one tends to produce the other. I have lived in Washington for four decades, and I have seen government agencies piled on top of government agencies to such an extent that even those responsible for their proper functioning can hardly determine the boundaries of their respective jurisdictions. Our government is dangerously top-heavy.

Accompanying the alarming growth of government, and perhaps as an inevitable concomitant, is a tendency on the part of the people to lean more and more on Washington.

That individuals and local communities should look more and more to the government for aid is deplorable. The only nation that can possibly be strong is the one that is strong "at the grass roots." The tendency to pile bureau on bureau, the endless drive of politicians to get their friends on the public payrolls, the tendency of bureaus to increase their own importance and their own size—all this is the equivalent of a disease.

Fascism is an amoral philosophy of government which thrives best where government has become too big. The main trouble with our world today is the extent to which governments have become the masters instead of the servants of their people. *The Washington Post* made the sage observation in a recent editorial that one of the reasons for high taxes is that so many people seek and obtain from the government so much more than government.

One who is trained to respect basic human rights, as a lawyer is supposed to be, is frightened by today's totalitarianism across the sea. The basic issue in the world today, as a lawyer sees it, is the issue of human freedom and the sanctity of man. The Russian type of Communism makes the government the master of its people and reduces man to a point where he is a mere cog in a huge superstate machine. In our beloved nation, thank God, government is still the servant; but we shall indeed be blind if we fail to see the danger to human freedom when government becomes too big, especially if contemporaneously there is a deliberate policy of encouraging the people to lean on government, as there has been at times.

While resisting Communism, as we must, and being suspicious of "fellow travelers," as we must, we should not close our eyes to the dangers of fascism. Freedom can be lost just as quickly under fascism as under Communism—perhaps faster. There was no control of Italy by Communists when Mussolini ruled with an iron hand. There was no Communism in Germany under Hitler. A few strong-willed individuals can seize power, especially if backed by the military, and set up their own government without regard to the will of the people. Mudslinging, lying, and character assassination are among the weapons which fascists use to gain power.

It was my privilege to study under Woodrow Wilson at Princeton. If any man ever had a fear of big government, it was he, and he imparted to us boys his fear of big government. He would point his finger at us and say: "Boys, be on your guard when you hear the voice of America coming from Washington. The real voice of America comes from the little farm, the little church, the little red schoolhouse, the little plant or factory, the places where men live and work and serve."

The gospel of hard work is such a vital part of my creed that, at the risk of repetition, I must treat it further. The freedom that we enjoy today would never have been possible without labor and struggle and blood and tears. It is a spiritual law that the good things of life shall not be easily attained. For that reason it causes me great concern to observe a tendency on the part of many people to do a minimum of work, to seek soft jobs, to assume that the government owes them a living, to stand in line waiting for relief checks when jobs are plentiful, to make rules that prohibit more than a minimum amount of work, to try to make a living out of gambling or speculation, to feed at the public trough.

One need not be an isolationist to be a passionate lover of America. We love its rocks and rills and templed hills, its great cities, "rock pillars of the state," its endless plains, the fields of waving grain—surely God never endowed another nation with such natural wealth. But we love even more America's fight for human freedom and the dignity of man. Our love for the Stars and Stripes is greater because of the invisible golden strands in our national emblem which represent love of God, respect for the Bible, a deep love for the church, hatred of tyranny, a passion for freedom and for justice, and an instinctive fear of too much government. Our flag stands for all these things, and it still floats high, not so much because of our merit but because of the sacrifices and the bloodshed of our forefathers.

This is not to say that our nation is perfect. We have only to consider our race prejudice, our liquor, our gambling, and our complacency in the face of world tragedy to see how far from Christ we are. Even our church is on the defensive in these days, and it should be, for it is to a large extent a class church, representing for the most part the middle class. We shall be avoiding reality if we fail to see all across the world the emergence of new classes, with the downtrodden asserting themselves, and with the decline of the *bourgeoisie* as a necessary corollary. Does the church have the genius to make itself a vital part of the life of all men so that it will love them and speak for them and lead them toward God? If not, it is my opinion that the church is doomed, for any institution that tries to keep itself on a class basis cannot withstand the onward march of the masses of men.

What we want for men generally is the blessings of a Christian democracy, in which they can own their own homes, have their own little gardens, and raise their own pigs, without fear that the government will take their pigs away from them and deny their right to plow their own land. To a great extent we have found freedom for all here, and we in America have made it possible for men to find the abundant life to a greater extent than it has been attained in any other nation.

But Christian laymen cannot go on hating people of other faiths and races and tolerating lynching and the poll tax and the Ku-Klux Klan and a nation saturated with liquor and gambling. Our Christian democracy will withstand Communism and dictatorship in proportion as it has the moral fiber to protect the dignity and the sanctity of all men and their economic and spiritual welfare.

We have a whale of a job to do if we are to stop the prairie fire that is sweeping across the world. We shall be very shortsighted if we think that we are protected from the same fire that is engulfing other nations. We can protect ourselves only in one way—by giving the masses of our own people a great faith in and a great love for Christian democracy. There need be no fear of the ravages of Communism, or even socialism, if the masses of our people have faith in the things that have made America great, in the Stars and Stripes as a symbol of human freedom, and in the genius of Christian America to keep everlastingly at the job of building a finer democracy.

We love the church because it helps to preserve the precious values which make a Christian democracy.

CHAPTER 8

Sacrificing for Love

"My heart an altar, and Thy love the flame."
—George Croly

We love the church for its sacrifice.

In instances almost without number I have seen men and women give to the church more than they can afford to give. I have seen tired women slave in hot church kitchens preparing meals for church dinners without monetary reward and solely because they love the church so much.

I have seen many women, overtired from a week's work, teach in the Sunday school or sing in the church choir solely because of their love for Jesus Christ and his church.

I have seen my mother bake eight cakes for a church cake sale when she was ill enough to be in bed.

I am thinking also of the brave missionaries at home and abroad, who labor with no thought of the cost.

I am thinking of a little church in the Philippines, its roof bombed away during the war, and of the devoted women who loved the church so much that they got together and made a canvas roof to cover the front part of the sanctuary; and of the doughboys who loved the same church so much that they finished the job with old tin. (Mission funds have since built a new roof for that church.)

I am thinking also of the day when our hydroplane dropped on the water on the poor little fishing village of Hoonah, Alaska—a strange village where all the homes are huddled together on a narrow ledge because there is no other place to build. Four years earlier the entire village, including the little church, had been destroyed by fire. Now the poor fishermen had rebuilt the whole village, including an attractive little church. The Indian pastor explained to me that poor fishing for several seasons had made the financing of the rebuilding very difficult, yet the people, in spite of their poverty, were determined to raise, in addition to the cost of the rebuilding program, their share of a national church fund which was being collected at the time! Tears almost came to my eyes when I realized how much those poor Indians loved the church, and with what true sacrifice they contributed their equivalent of the widow's mite.

When I think of the hardship of our missionaries at home and abroad, and of their pitifully inadequate salaries, and of the ministers who are bravely carrying on although there is not enough money available in the family treasury for needed clothing, I frankly wonder why our love for the church seems to be so much less than theirs, when measured by the inadequate sacrifice which most of us laymen make for our Lord.

My plea to every layman is that he will conscientiously rethink the question of stewardship, asking himself, Does my contribution to the church adequately reflect the extent of my love for Christ and his church?

Jesus gave his all. He is less interested in the giving of our money than in the giving of our hearts. But I suspect that if we are holding back on the giving of money, we are holding back on something far more important. For where love is fervent, it will express itself in terms of sacrifice. In the whole realm of religion there is nothing more important than the willingness of the disciple to spend himself and spend his money for Jesus Christ. It is this pouring out of self until it hurts that marks the true Christian.

In the last analysis it all comes back to the question of love. If we love Christ and his church enough, we will not stay away from church for light reasons. If we love enough, we will not easily turn down a church committee assignment. If we love enough, we will not refuse to help in the church school or the choir. If we love enough, we will not have too tight a hold on our pocketbooks. Love wants to pour itself out. Love never counts the cost. Love never fails.

"The greatest of these is love."

CHAPTER 9

When Trouble Comes

"Only when we have faith can we be free from fear. If you are afraid, then we must suspect that you have no faith."

—Peter Marshall

We love the church for its tender ministry when trouble comes.

The church unfailingly sends its messengers to the bedside in the name of the Great Physician. It is the minister or priest whom the family first calls when the dark shadow of death falls. But best of all, it is the church that brings hope when all is despair, and the light of Jesus Christ when all is darkness.

Without the church the person who is seriously ill—perhaps facing a major operation—is apt to be dominated by fear. The church substitutes faith for fear.

Our mortal bodies, miracles though they are, are subject to illness and disintegration when viewed from a human standpoint. But even death becomes the gateway to a higher life when viewed from God's standpoint.

One's attitude toward sickness depends on one's faith. If God really engineers the circumstances of those who love him, there is no reason to fear illness, for he is in charge of our situation in sickness as well as in health. God is in the valleys of life as well as on the mountaintops.

It is not on the mountaintops that we can best glorify God, according to Oswald Chambers, but in "the drab drudgery of the valley." It is easy to have faith in God when our path is rosy and all is well with us, but the test comes in the dark valleys of life where we encounter setbacks, discouragements, illness, and the death of dear ones. Will God seem as real and as good to us then as he seemed on the heights? We like to think of ourselves mounting up with wings of eagles—it tickles our ego to picture ourselves soaring among life's mountain peaks; but according to Chambers it is as important to know how to come down as to know how to ascend, and "the power of the saint lies in the coming down and the living down."

Jesus made it very clear that each of us will have his own cross to carry. It may not be like Jesus' cross, but it will be real. It may consist of financial loss, business troubles, illness, bereavement, misunderstanding, loneliness. It requires faith, courage, and sacrifice to bear such burdens. The glory of the Christian faith is that it gives us the grace to carry any kind of cross, because Jesus helps us carry it. Many a brave Christian have I seen stand up nobly under terrible business strain. Many a brave woman I have seen holding fast to her faith in the face of hopeless conditions.

Is there anything finer known to men than a faith that will enable us to stand confident and even victorious in the face of adversity? Such a faith is more precious than gold, "yea, than much fine gold: sweeter also than honey and the honeycomb."

Blessed is the layman or laywoman who has learned the meaning of Christian sacrifice, and who can say fervently:

> Nearer, my God, to Thee,
> Nearer to Thee!
> E'en though it be a cross
> That raiseth me.[1]

Jesus did not spend his time laughing and rejoicing. He had his hours of trial and tears. The Christian life is an upward struggle toward ultimate peace, but it is not a perpetual picnic.

When the "blue" hours come, use them for quiet communion with God. Don't make the mistake of trying artificially to act happy and exuberant. Don't worry about the days when you are ill or feel "down." Worry only when you have no longing for the touch of God's hand.

Cardinal Newman was lost on a sailing ship in the Mediterranean when, with a faith that will shine through the ages, he wrote:

> Lead, kindly Light, amid the encircling gloom,
> Lead Thou me on!
> The night is dark, and I am far from home;
> Lead Thou me on!

Driving to work on a recent rainy morning, I offered a ride to a woman and her four-year-old son. As they got into the car, I caught a glimpse of her face—a face in which a quiet faith seemed literally to shine. I spoke to the boy, but he did not respond. "I am sorry," said the young mother. "Harold has been deaf from birth, and his deafness, I am told, is incurable."

Then I learned that her cowardly husband, upon learning that the boy would always be deaf, had left his wife stranded and helpless, except for her great faith in Jesus Christ. Now she carries on alone, still

[1] Sarah F. Adams.

teaching in Sunday school, and living on modest alimony. "It is not easy," she said, "but I love Harold the more because it is not easy. God never fails, you know."

Those blessed words from a brave woman left stranded with a deaf son continue to ring in my ears, and I know they will give me strength when strength is needed.

"Yea, though I walk through the valley of the shadow of death, I will fear no evil: for thou art with me; thy rod and thy staff they comfort me."

The last sentence is precious. "Thy rod and thy staff, they comfort me." Shepherds always carry a long rod or staff reaching high into the air. The sheep in the rear of the flock often lose sight of the shepherd, but they are never afraid as long as they can see the tall rod or staff. So we human beings often seem to lose our hold on God, but if we will look up, we are apt to find something pointing to him—perhaps the voice of a brave woman saying, "God never fails, you know."

Of the sayings of our Master one of the most precious is this: "Blessed are the poor in spirit: for theirs is the kingdom of heaven." Our Lord knew, as no man ever did, the struggles which take place within the human soul. It is inevitable that a good man shall be depressed and discouraged at times. The very striving of an earnest person to square his life with God's will may cause distress of soul, especially if the striving is less successful than one would wish. The more sensitive the individual, the greater will be his spiritual distress. Such a one is discouraged, and "poor in spirit."

But the great sympathetic heart of Jesus understands it all. He knows that the souls thus battling with themselves are closer to God than are those who take life lightly and who do not care enough about God to allow a conflict to rage within themselves. A priest has well said that "suffering may be the path to glory." It is possible that we are closer to God when we are sick or discouraged over our lack of spiritual progress than when we are riding on top of the world with a Pollyanna exuberance. Certain it is that we draw closer and closer to him as we fight down the things within us that are in conflict with his will. If the battle for the right gets us down now and then, we shall find consolation in the fact that it is the poor in spirit who shall inherit the kingdom of heaven.

An aged friend from Texas who formerly lived in a lovely New England village writes: "My son wants me to join this big Texas church, but I don't want to do it, because my heart is still with the little white church in New England. I love it so much that I want to be buried there."

A little white church in New England comforting an elderly lady in Texas! The love that emanates from a little church can reach over great distances. It can reach beyond the seas to far-flung battle lines where young men who do not know how soon they will be killed read their little Testament which their church has given them. Their hearts are warmed as they think of the ties back home and of what the little church has meant to them.

The church helps us to keep a right perspective when trouble comes. Without the valleys of life there could be no hills. Without the sunset there would be no sunrise. Without the night there would be no morning. The church helps us to look up to the hills when we are lost in the valleys and to know that the darkest night is followed by the dawn.

One of the world's leading psychiatrists, after studying literally hundreds of neurotic patients, observed as to the patients over thirty-five years of age that "there has not been one whose problem in the last resort has not been that of finding a religious outlook on life." [2] This is just another way of saying that when men lose God, they find themselves mentally adrift, just as a ship which has lost its propeller drifts helplessly. It is God who gives life its energy, its direction, and its unity. It is religion that ties the loose ends of life together. Is it any wonder, then, that when men lose God and religion, their life tends to disintegrate? It is indeed significant that a noted psychiatrist should put his finger on "a religious outlook on life" as the one factor that was missing in his ailing patients. It is the church, of course, and the church alone that can supply this missing factor.

There is no trouble so deep that God cannot reach it, no wound so serious that the Great Physician cannot heal it, no night so dark that God cannot dispel it with the dawn.

"God never fails, you know."

[2] Carl G. Jung, *Modern Man in Search of a Soul* (New York: Harcourt, Brace and Co., 1933).

CHAPTER 10

Missions

"And he said unto them, Go ye into all the world, and preach the gospel to every creature."

—Mark 16:15

We love the church for its service to humanity and to Christ through Christian missions.

One of the greatest dangers confronting the church is that the church will serve itself instead of serving humanity. "For a true church must live a pilgrim life upon the road of God's unfolding purpose, keeping close to the rugged boundaries of his ever-expanding Kingdom." [1]

It is high time for laymen to take the cause of missions more seriously. It is a legitimate criticism of the church that its missionary program has been supported too largely by women and not largely enough by men. Without belittling in the least the very important work which women have done and are still doing in the field of missions, it must be said with the utmost frankness that a large part of the missionary effort requires masculine, rather than feminine, support.

Christian men must be placed in key positions in governments across the sea and the whole policy of governments changed. Frank Laubach, noted Christian missionary, warns us, for example, that India stands at the crossroads today, one road leading to Communism and another to Christianity. The next few years will decide. And, warns Dr. Laubach, as goes India, so go Africa and the whole Near East.

Not only is there a tremendous job to do in the field of missions, but it is such a difficult job that it will require the best we have in Christian statesmanship. One thinks, for example, of the tragic situation in the Near East, where Arab is poised against Jew and where the very Holy Land of Bible days is now split in two by forces which despise each other. One dares not travel the direct road between Jerusalem and Bethlehem today, so forbidding is the line of demarcation which has been drawn between the land of the Arabs and the land of the Jews.

So serious is this problem that the best statesmanship of the world

[1] Message to American Christians issued by National Council of Churches at its Denver Conference, 1952.

has thus far been unable to solve it. The big question of the day is whether Christianity can solve it. One thing is sure: It cannot be solved by our contributing to all church benevolences less than two cents per day per member.[2]

Every Christian missionary station throughout the world is a fortress of Christ's far-flung battle line. The Communists have their missionaries to preach hatred and destruction. It is frightening to think of the gravity of the issue and of the dangerous inadequacy of our missionary personnel and equipment. We laymen are very foolish indeed if we do not recognize the thinness of Christianity's missionary battle line, the danger which it involves for our Christian civilization, and the need of masculine support to strengthen it.

Not many years ago laymen were often heard to express doubt about the value of missions. But not in this day, for laymen are beginning to see that their very freedom may hinge on the success of our missionary effort. For if the world is won by the damnable ideology of Communism, which already has resulted in the enslavement of whole nations and in the imprisonment of ministers and priests, and if the way of Jesus Christ does not prevail, then I submit that everything is lost.

We laymen must get a fresh understanding of the vital importance of every local church, of every church school, of every Christian college, of every missionary station. For these institutions and the consecrated souls who are manning them are holding a battle line which protects all that we hold dear. It is up to Christian laymen to decide whether the battle line will hold.

Jesus was talking to us laymen when he said: "Go ye into all the world, and preach the gospel to every creature." God must be displeased with us laymen, and with some ministers, for surrendering this vitally important sector of Christ's battle line. If our Christian civilization is to be saved, we must throw red-blooded men against the enemy and support them with ample money and with prayers.

It is gratifying to report that Christian statesmen now occupy many key positions in foreign governments, and that our missionary schools and colleges throughout the world are making a heavy impact on the policies of nations. At this very moment the government of South Korea is calling for more Christian missionaries, and Communist prisoners from China and North Korea are being led to Christ by the hundreds in the prison camps of the United Nations, south of the

[2] This is the official figure for the year 1952 for a leading Protestant denomination.

thirty-eighth parallel. Not a few of the Asiatic leaders, including Madame Chiang Kai-shek, are graduates of American colleges.

Syngman Rhee, President of South Korea, is a Christian. Said he to Harold E. Fey, of *The Christian Century:* "The influence of the million Christians in Korea is felt everywhere—in the Government of the National Assembly, in the country as a whole. . . . Christianity brings great strength to a nation."

Carlos P. Romulo, ambassador from the Philippines and one of the great international statesmen of our day, is an outstanding Christian who recently presided over a meeting of the General Assembly of the United Nations. The new minister of education in the government of South Korea is George Paik, a graduate of Princeton Theological Seminary. Although Pakistan is a Moslem nation, its new minister to the United States is a Christian. Dr. Charles Malik, Lebanon's minister to the United States, is a product of one of our mission schools in Tripoli and of our university in Beirut. Says Malik: "I knew all the missionaries and they were God-fearing men and women, sincere, humble, hard-working." Allah Yar Saleh, ambassador from Iran to the United States, although not a baptized Christian, is described as "Christian in ideal and outlook." Of the two commissioners in the Punjab state of India one is a Christian, as is also one of the deputy commissioners. The governor of the state of Bombay, Raja Sir Maharaj Singh, is a Christian whose first act when he became governor was to order that no liquor should be served in the governor's mansion. The governor of Bombay and the health minister of the Central Government of India are both children of the first moderator of the United Church of Northern India.

The list might be indefinitely continued.[3] These examples are cited merely to show what intelligent missionary effort can accomplish. We laymen must realize that it is impossible to build a Christian world unless we can put into public office throughout the world public officials with clear Christian insights. Such men are being molded every day by our fine Christian schools and colleges in every part of the world.

In the field of health our missionary effort is of tremendous importance. Fighting against ignorance, Christian medical missionaries are at work on every continent. They have carried a healing ministry of love into the Far East, the Near East, Africa, and Latin America to lay the foundations upon which governments are being built. Meanwhile, our

[3] A list subsequently received from Dr. W. N. Wysham of Christians occupying government positions in India is so long that it cannot be reproduced here, but it is an inspiring list.

missionaries are training young people from kindergarten through college and conditioning their hearts for public service in China, Korea, Japan, the Philippines, Siam, India, and Burma.

The church of Jesus Christ is slowly but surely leavening the total lump of humanity with the consciousness of its high call to brotherhood in Jesus Christ.

As important as foreign missions is the missionary effort within our own nation. It is disturbing to think that in the greatest democracy of the world there are literally millions of people who do not acknowledge Christ and other millions who, although they acknowledge him, are denied the opportunity for Christian worship.

It was my privilege to study our missionary program in Alaska, that great territory which occupies a strategic position between Siberia and the United States. My heart was touched when I saw Indian boys and girls of high-school age studying in their classrooms and looking just as clean and bright as any of the boys and girls in our American high schools. And tears actually came to my eyes when I heard a group of Eskimo men and women sing "Since Jesus Came into My Heart."

Alaska is still a frontier, and it has many unlovely characteristics of frontier life, including liquor and gambling. The hold which liquor has on Alaska—thanks to the American liquor industry—is so strong as to shock the conscience of any citizen, church member or not. I fervently thanked God, as I traveled through Alaska, that the missionaries and mission stations of the church are there to teach the Indians and the Eskimos that there is a kind of life that is better than the life given to liquor and gambling. The church is the only hope of Alaska.

Romantic chapters could be written also about missionary efforts in the mountain areas, among the Indians, and in our great cities. Our national missions program strives to make America a Christian nation, that it may better serve the world. It must be apparent to Christian laymen that the success of our foreign missionary program, on which the whole future of our Christian culture may depend, must necessarily hinge largely on our success in Christianizing our own nation.

CHAPTER 11

Prayer

"Love God and God's love can enfold you and energize you and enlighten you and purify you and make you more than conquerors."

—Albert E. Day

Prayer is our only means of direct communication with God. The truly abundant life cannot be attained without that communication with the Source of all life and of all good.

There is nothing in the whole field of religion that is less understood by laymen than prayer, yet nothing is more important.

Through prayer we maintain a loving contact with our God. Through prayer we get the strength to cope with the trials and tribulations of life and to live confidently and triumphantly, because we are in his loving hands and because our little life has become part of a divine pattern. Through prayer we obtain forgiveness for any wrong we have done, and we get a new start. Through prayer we lift our human sights toward higher goals. Through prayer we eliminate from our lives the things which separate us from God. Through prayer we turn sorrow into joy and defeat into victory. Through prayer we lay hold of a power far greater than our own, a power equal to every need. Through prayer we transform and energize our lives by making Jesus Christ a vital part of our daily living.

I can say from my personal experience that prayer is not always easy. To condition ourselves properly for prayer there must be real soul searching and faithful checking up on our own life and behavior. Prayer is not effective if we are poorly conditioned for it. The trouble with us laymen is that we are human, and therefore subject to all human temptations—the temptation to be selfish, the tempation to be quick-tempered, the temptation to advance ourselves, the temptation to enjoy forbidden fruits. How can we expect to lay hold of God in prayer as long as we willfully violate his laws? It is only when we say, "I am sorry," and mean it, that God becomes real to us, and that prayer becomes effective.

The point at which most of us laymen are most in need of prayer is the point at which our affections must be controlled. It is so very difficult for us to tear from our hearts the love of false gods which we shamefully allow to compete with Jesus Christ.

> The dearest idol I have known,
> Whate'er that idol be,
> Help me to tear it from Thy throne,
> And worship only Thee.[1]

Prayer is the means by which we seek to raise ourselves up toward God and try to get a better understanding of his will in our lives. Sometimes I wish that there might be no other type of prayer than the one in which we seek to cleanse ourselves, to get out of our lives everything that is inconsistent with God's purpose, to get ourselves in tune with him. "Create in me a clean heart, O God; and renew a right spirit within me." For, after all, the object of all prayer and of all religion is to draw men closer to God. It is only by nurturing the spiritual side of our nature through prayer that we can keep ourselves sensitive to the higher things, that we can attain a sensitivity "that will love mercy and justice and goodness *the world around* and within the local community; that will cherish beauty and seek its harmony and wholeness in living; that will look to wisdom and find its sovereign source." [2]

The kind of prayer that means most to me is the simple prayer that comes right from the heart:

"God, help me to eliminate from my life anything that is inconsistent with thy will." What a prayer that is if we really mean it!

"God, help me to live confidently and unafraid because my trust is in thee."

"God, help me to understand what it means to be a disciple of Jesus Christ."

"God, help me in my daily living to be a Christian example to others."

"Father, make me always conscious of thy presence with me, and let my every word and act take thee into account."

"Forgive, dear God, the inadequacy of my discipleship."

These are but a few illustrations of the type of prayer that means most to me. Such prayers are packed with power if they are made with sincerity, for

> Prayer is the soul's sincere desire
> Uttered or unexpressed;

[1] William Cowper.

[2] Bernard E. Meland, *Seeds of Redemption* (New York: The Macmillan Co., 1947), p. 10.

The motion of a hidden fire,
That trembles in the breast.[3]

It is a great mistake to look upon prayer as a means of getting personal gain. God is not a Santa Claus. Petition for self-gain is a low form of prayer.

Prayer accomplishes little unless we are willing to do our part. The man who sits with folded hands and does nothing to help himself cannot expect God to do much for him. Dr. Sockman hits the nail on the head: "In bringing our wishes to God, it sometimes happens that the divine door remains closed until we do something with our hands, as the man did who went and knocked." [4]

God wants us to do our best. He wants us to be good, to be clean, to be honorable, and to do our utmost for ourselves. If we are not doing our best, how can we expect God to help us? Dr. Sockman is right: the door may remain closed to us unless we are worthy of having it opened. One of our great ministers, John Sutherland Bonnell, says that "we have become soft and self-indulgent in our outlook on religion." [5] If this is true, as it surely is, how can we expect God to pay much attention to our prayers?

The right kind of prayer is a process of attuning, a spiritual and mental house cleaning, a conscious surrender of the will, a dedication of self to God. The process of attuning brings about what Dr. Day calls a "heightening of sensitivity" to the things of God. I like this expression because it is so necessary for the church to get hold of callous, indifferent, and lukewarm laymen and make them more sensitive to the higher things. Given enough prayer, the erstwhile indifferent layman learns really to love Jesus Christ and his church; and if he remains constant in prayer, the day is sure to come when he can say warmly: "My heart an altar, and Thy love the flame."

When we have straightened our own lives out through prayer, we are ready for the highest form of prayer—namely, intercessory prayer. There is real danger that we laymen will spend so much time praying for ourselves that we forget others. Oh, how we laymen should be praying in these tragic days for other people; for the millions who are putting up a brave struggle against poverty; for the multitudes who

[3] James Montgomery, "Prayer."

[4] Ralph W. Sockman, *The Higher Happiness* (New York and Nashville: Abingdon-Cokesbury Press, 1950), p. 93.

[5] *What Are You Living For?* (New York and Nashville: Abingdon-Cokesbury Press, 1950), p. 91.

live under the cruel handicap of race prejudice; for the other millions in concentration camps; for the millions whose minds are enslaved; for the other millions who do not know Jesus Christ! Christ's plea to us is that we shall bring others to him.

Am I wrong in feeling that the church lays less emphasis on personal praying than it did a generation ago? The prayer meeting seems to be dying out, and I fear that nothing is being substituted for it. It seems that the church is failing at this point, for if church members do not pray, they simply cannot be good disciples. The clear duty of the church is to bring men to God, and this cannot be done without prayer. A consecrated layman has said: "The degree to which a church can be said to be doing its job is determined by how well and how consistently it gives direction and help to its people in this search after God."

It is possible to reach a point where prayer becomes as much a part of life as breathing, and everything is then done in the spirit of prayer. I covet for laymen the type of Christian living in which Christ is in every letter that is written, in every family circle, in every meal that is eaten, in every personal contact during the day, in every classroom, in every sale that is made, in every plowing of a field, in every hearing in the courtroom.

As Dr. Albert E. Day so beautifully points out,[6] God does not care about the *words* with which we pray. What he does care about is our *attitudes*. The bending of our will toward his will; the earnest desire to know him better; the feeling of utter helplessness without him; the sense of awe that is caused by a right appreciation of the miracles of life; a real love for Jesus Christ, his Son; a penitent recognition of the inadequacy of our discipleship—these are the kind of things God really loves, and they add up to the prayer life.

[6] I would express my personal indebtedness to Dr. Day for his stimulating book *The Autobiography of Prayer* (New York: Harper & Bros., 1952).

CHAPTER 12

Our Homes and Our Youth

"If we could have a great multitude of young people forming their vision of the future in loyalty to Christ and then giving themselves heart and soul, in the power of his spirit, to bring the vision true, there is no limit to what we might accomplish for our country and through it for the world."

—William Temple

The very heart of Christian America is the home. We love the church because it builds homes in which every member is the servant of every other member, in which love reigns, and in which Jesus Christ is always accepted as a member of the family.

My gratitude to God is very great because I was blessed with truly Christian parents and because even as a boy I was made to feel the unseen presence of Christ in our home. For our home was one in which a gracious and loving atmosphere always prevailed. Hardly a single harsh word do I remember, even though nerves must often have been tense in those early years because of economic hardship. I often wonder whether there is any more valuable characteristic in all the world than the grace to bear adversity with a smile. My parents had that grace in abundant measure, and they could accept good fortune and ill fortune alike as God's will.

So active were my parents in the church that the church always seemed to be an integral part of our family life. Father was a church officer and had a large class of girls in the Sunday school. Mother was president of the missionary society, sang in the choir, and taught in the Sunday school. For the family to walk to church on Sunday morning was as natural and inevitable as for the day to follow the night, and our attendance at Sunday school was regular. I joined the church when I was twelve years old. The minister who made the deepest impression on my boyhood heart was Harlan G. Mendenhall, a sweet and gentle soul who always seemed to me to have the sensitive, loving touch of the Saviour. Many a time did I say to myself, "Jesus must have been like that."

Very noticeable to me as a child was the Christian love between my father and mother. In those years the health of both parents was such as to call for loving care, for Mother suffered from a severe stomach ailment and Father from headaches caused by business pressure. Each parent had to play nurse to the other, and this was done with a fidelity and love which could not escape us boys.

On the hall of our living room hung a motto, embroidered in red silk, which Grandmother had given to Mother soon after Mother's wedding. It read: "What is home without a mother?" This reminded all of us constantly of the importance of the mother in the household. It is she who must bear the main burden of looking after the children. It is she who must look after all details of food, clothing, laundry, and the thousand and one little duties that tend to wear a mother out. Young children, bless their little hearts, can be as mischievous and contrary and "ornery" as anything on this earth, and the mother is supposed, in the midst of all of it, and beset by endless household duties, to be calm and serene, an example of Christian poise and faith. This my mother was able to do in spite of ill health, and I have never ceased to love her and almost worship her for it.

The Church and Juvenile Delinquency

In later years I was to see the sorrows and the heartaches that are caused by the absence of a Christian atmosphere in the home. It was my privilege to be for twelve years a member of a board of parole, passing on thousands of cases of youthful offenders.

Nothing in my experience on the board of parole impressed me more than the very small number of delinquency cases from Christian homes. When a boy who had a church background came before our board, we raised our eyebrows and commented on it, so rare was it to see a criminal offender from a truly Christian environment. What a tribute to Christianity it is that our youthful offenders come almost wholly from non-Christian homes!

Never shall I forget a certain young man who was before our board for parole on a larceny charge. He looked pale and beaten, and his record for larceny was unusually bad, so parole was almost automatically denied. But I could hardly sleep that night for thinking about him, and I decided to visit his home. There I learned that his father was an alcoholic and his mother was in jail for bootlegging. His frail young sister was home alone when I called, bearing on her young shoulders the burdens and the troubles that inevitably come when the laws of God are violated. My visit resulted in a new plan under which the young man was paroled to live with an aunt in another jurisdiction, where he resumed his schooling and got into no further trouble.

Twelve years on a board of parole convinced me that a church is better protection to a community than a score of jails and that there is no better protection to our youth than a Christian home.

As I studied the young men and young women who came before us as criminal offenders, I reached another firm conviction—namely, that many of the young offenders get into trouble because they have no one to love them. My experience abundantly confirms the opinion of a real expert in criminology which I quote:

> A child who is not loved is insecure. Too often a child who has never been loved or wanted finds it difficult to accept and love others. Unfortunately, he may develop a strong need to get even for being unwanted, with a resulting hostility towards society, and refusal to accept social standards. The rejected child of today develops into the criminal of tomorrow.[1]

The lives of children can be warped by too rigid discipline and by too much scolding. On the other hand, lack of discipline is sure to cause weakness and irresponsibility in the child. Fortunate is the parent who is able to combine discipline and love in such a way as to make the child feel that the discipline is the equivalent of loving guidance. Nervous scolding is not loving guidance, nor is too much strictness. It is in the Christian home that the child will develop normally, because in such a home love dominates, and discipline is simply a part of the love pattern.

If your boy or girl and mine are really loved, if there are loving arms to which they are sure they can fly when trouble comes, if they have the sense of security that comes from being loved, there is not much reason to fear that they will get into criminal difficulties. Where Christ is the unseen member of the family circle, there is a guaranty that normal, fruitful, and happy lives will result. We love the church because it holds out that assurance.

A word of caution may not be out of place regarding disagreements between father and mother in the home. Children are quick to sense intuitively any strained relationships in the family which tend to produce a feeling of insecurity in the offspring. An unconscionable amount of damage is done in the home by harsh words and by scolding, both often caused by selfishness or by nervous tension.

We love the church because it helps to build homes where love reigns and where children are brought up to love Jesus Christ and his church.

[1] H. S. Lippman, "Emotional Factors in Juvenile Delinquency," *Proceedings of the American Prison Associaton,* 1938, pp. 271, 276.

When I visit a church for the first time and desire to form an opinion as to its effectiveness, I do not pay much attention to the size of the congregation or of the plant, or to the amount of the church budget. I always look first for the vigor and success of the work with young people. Show me a church that is alive with young people, and I will show you a successful church. Show me a church that has in it mostly adults and only a few young peope, and I will show you a church that is static, if not decadent.

I have studied the young people of today at close range, and I have every confidence in them. Those pessimists who feel that the young people of this generation are inferior morally and otherwise to the young people of earlier generations know not whereof they speak. The boys and girls of today are, on the whole, alert, intelligent, and eager for the truth in spiritual matters. They are spiritually ahead of where my generation stood at their age.

I consider myself better qualified than are most adults to pass upon the quality of our young people because I am only seventeen years of age. When I met with a splendid group of young people in California, all of whom were members of the Westminster Fellowship and of an average age of seventeen, they wanted to elect me a member of the Fellowship, but my age was a bar—men over sixty are not eligible to join! So they went through a painfully formal ceremony, cutting the years off my age one at a time with a carving knife until they got me down to seventeen, whereupon they elected me a life member of the Fellowship. For this reason I consider myself specially qualified to understand the hopes, the aspirations, and the problems of other teenagers like myself.

One of the most eloquent speeches I have heard during the last few years was made by a young college girl on her return from the great International Christian Youth Conference in Oslo, Norway, where Christian young people from all over the world gathered in a great international assembly. This young lady opened our eyes to a great vision of universal brotherhood and thrilled us by her eloquence. I cannot quote her whole speech, but I do remember one small part of it: "As we sat around the communion table in Norway, young people of white skin, black skin, brown skin, and yellow skin, joining hands as we prayed together, we did not have the feeling that we were there *studying* the Church universal—we felt that we *were* the Church universal." Sometimes I wonder whether we older people have as real a vision of world brotherhood as our young people have. How thrilling it is to think that the church is giving them an appreciation of God and a vision of a great world community in Jesus Christ!

There is hope and encouragement in the eagerness with which youth approach the subject of religion. Their inquisitiveness is a healthy sign. They are earnestly seeking after the truth.

I fear that in the days of my youth the feeling prevailed, if indeed it was not encouraged by our elders, that the Christian religion was to be accepted without asking too many questions about it. We were to accept it "on faith," which too often meant that we were not to think too keenly about it. This is, of course, fatal, because any faith that cannot be justified by the minds and consciences which God has given us is not worth having. The Christian religion can stand any amount of questioning, and our youth should be encouraged to ask questions. Our responsibility is to answer them. Professor Doescher says that "there is no greater sin committed against young minds than to force them into the false dilemma of having to choose between Christian faith and mental honesty." [2]

The search for truth may of course lead one temporarily astray. There can be no courageous exploration without some danger of becoming lost. Nevertheless the honest and independent person must persevere in his search for truth. If we have confidence that our faith will stand the light, then we should encourage our young folk to approach religion not with a closed mind, but with a wide-open and eager mind. For it is the honest, open, and eager mind that really gets a grip on the laws of God and on the power of Jesus Christ to redeem the human soul. The mind that is closed cannot have more than a questionable grip on anything.

To a young person who earnestly seeks to find God I would suggest these steps from my own experience and the experience of Christians whom I greatly admire:

1. Make up your mind to strive honestly and earnestly for religious truth. An honestly open mind is a prerequisite.

2. Use your intellect to discover evidence of the reality of God in nature, in the lives of good men, in the Bible, within yourself.

3. Study to learn what men call the laws of God, and apply yourself diligently to the study of Jesus Christ and his gospel.

4. As the principles and the laws of God are unfolded to you, use your will power to apply them to your own life.

5. Think about your own nature, including your natural impulse to-

[2] "Natural Science and Christian Theology," *Theology Today*, IX (October, 1952), No. 3, 315.

ward sin, and ask yourself honestly whether your life does not need to be redeemed.

6. Study to learn the saving power of Jesus Christ through God's grace, and try to understand what it means to be "a new person" in Jesus Christ.

7. Remember, there is no ready-made device for finding God. You must surround yourself with Christian friends, read the Bible and other good literature, and associate yourself with the church. Don't hunt for God in the sky. Search for him in the hearts of good people, and learn to feel him in life's experience.

8. Pray hard that you may live up to your highest and best and that God through his love and grace will lead you to Jesus Christ.

This method has worked for millions, and it will work for you. Don't worry if you have doubts—if you are intellectually honest, there will be periods of doubt. Honest doubts are the steppingstones to faith. The doubts disappear as you get a better understanding of God's love, his grace, his infinite goodness, and the saving power of Jesus Christ. If you will follow this course honestly and earnestly and prayerfully, you will begin to feel increasingly the power of God in your life, and you will fall in love with Jesus Christ and accept him as the Lord and Master of your life.

The result of this method? The abundant life, peace of mind, a happy home, a fruitful life, a life that brings untold blessings to others as God uses you as his instrument, and at last, salvation and eternal life.

Is it not worth trying if it has worked for millions?

A distressing feature of present-day Protestantism is the parsimonious support which most of the communions give to their colleges. In my own denomination our colleges are supported on what may fairly be called a "shoestring basis," only five or ten thousand dollars a year for each institution out of a total income of half a million or more. Since there can be no adequate citizenship without education, and since Christian education is doubly needed in such a day as this, our default in this vital matter is enough to make a strong man weep.

Many times I have thanked God for the religious foundations or fellowships in our universities. These are doubly needed because of the trend toward secularism in the field of education. When boys and girls leave home to go to college, they face one of the most critical periods of life. Every Christian parent breathes a sigh of relief when informed that his or her boy or girl has become part of such a group in a university, for it means that God will not be lost as the young man or woman embarks on what is almost a new life.

Horace Mann, a true lover of young people, said:

> If, suddenly summoned to eternity, I were able to give but one parting word of advice to my own children, or to the children of others;—if I were sinking beneath the wave, and had time to utter but one articulate breath, or were wasting away upon the death-bed, and had strength to make but one exhortation more,—that dying legacy should be, "Remember thy Creator in the days of thy youth."

CHAPTER 13

Christian Friendship

"Our work and our friends give us help and the triangle of God, others, and self is made complete."

—Eugene Exman

Among all the many wonderful blessings which a loving God has showered upon us, none is greater than the blessing of friendship.

A person cannot live a normal life alone. The joys of life must be shared with others, and when the sorrows and heartaches come, we need friends to help us bear them. God in his infinite wisdom has mercifully arranged matters in such a way that we need not bear our troubles alone.

The world knows no comfort greater than that of a loving hand slipped into ours when sorrow comes. Often it is not necessary that a single word be spoken, so deep is the understanding between those who love each other and who feel close to each other. Nothing is more eloquent or more comforting than the silence between two souls that are in tune, one with the other.

It is not even necessary that our friend be physically present with us, for the mere knowledge that he is our friend and that he loves us is enough to sustain us. Miles cannot really separate those who love each other, for love defies space.

However great may be the beauty of human love, it cannot match divine love. Jesus has taught us in a very beautiful way that even if human friends fail, we can lean upon him. "Come unto me, all ye that labour and are heavy laden, and I will give you rest." Life is made much easier and the burdens of life made much lighter if we develop the habit of thinking of Jesus as an intimate and loving partner who travels with us along the pathways of life.

The minister of our local church tells a beautiful story to illustrate how God helps us through other people and how help comes from above when we need it. Dr. Hollister speaks of the eleventh chapter of Matthew, in which Jesus speaks these beautiful words of comfort: "Take my yoke upon you, and learn of me; for I am meek and lowly in heart: and ye shall find rest unto your souls. For my yoke is easy, and my burden is light."

Many laymen have had difficulty with this passage because a yoke is usually thought of as a burden. But our minister tells of a canoe trip in the course of which he came to a "carry" across a rather difficult little hill. He was carrying his heavy canoe on his shoulders—no easy task on a hot day. Before he reached the top of the hill, he was perspiring freely and almost out of breath, and his shoulders were beginning to ache. At the top of the hill was a little cabin, and an old man was leaning against a gate. He looked sympathetically at the overburdened traveler and called out, "Where is your yoke?"

"My what?" asked the minister.

"Your yoke. Come around back here and I'll show you."

He led the fatigued minister to the rear of his cabin and fitted onto his shoulders a wooden yoke, specially designed for the carrying of canoes. When the canoe was lifted into place on the yoke, it could be carried with the greatest of ease—no more aching shoulders. Jesus does not tell us that we shall have no burdens to bear; burdens are a necessary part of any fruitful life. But he invites us to use his yoke to make the burdens lighter; and his yoke is always ready for us if we will but ask. We followers should never be without that yoke, for it helps us over all the rough places of life. It is not made of wood, like the canoe yoke, but it is made of infinite love and infinite power. For this reason it never fails, and no burden is too great for it.

There is nothing worse in this world than loneliness. Without friends a person almost "eats his heart out." If there is any person in the world who needs God's help, it is the lonely person. The church is a blessed refuge which God has provided for the lonely. For in the church there will always be a warm welcome, a friendly handclasp, and, if needed, a kindly and patient counselor.

I want real friends. I am not the backslapping type who tries to convert every man into a friend. I'd rather have a dozen real friends whose aims and purposes are the same as mine, who will visit me when I am sick and help me when I am in trouble and miss me when I am away, than a thousand to slap me on the back and say, "How about a little drink?" My wife and I find that our closest and dearest friends are to be found among the Christian people of the nation's capital and especially those in our own church. The value of these friendships cannot be measured, or even thought of, in terms of money. Ordinary friendship is wonderful, but friendship has a special value if the parties to it are bound together by the golden ties of Christian love. For then the friendship tends to take on something of a divine nature, and God can be felt in it. Love becomes more of a miracle when infinite love is interwoven with it. I love the church for the almost divine friendships which I have found within it.

Friendship should mean more to all of us because of the jittery condition of the world. We need one another more. The friendly handclasp means more. The kindly touch has a deeper meaning. We should place a higher value on friendship in such a time as this, understandings between friends should be more intimate, loving thoughts should bind friends more closely together, and Christ should be more real.

CHAPTER 14

The Church Music

"The world of man which came to its birth in music, when 'the morning stars sang together and the sons of God shouted for joy,' will end in a redemptive harmony."

—John A. Mackay

We love the church for its music, and especially for its hymns.

The ministry of a choir can be as effective as that of the pulpit. In a real sense every member of a choir is a minister, carrying the gospel in a beautiful way to all who hear. When at a recent church service a lovely soprano voice sang "I Walked Today Where Jesus Walked," I wondered if it would be possible to bring Jesus nearer to people than he was brought by that wonderful solo.

Perhaps it is because my dear mother was a choir member most of her life that I look upon the church choir as a vital part of the church. It has always seemed to me that there is something divine about music. All God's universe is a great harmony, and music symbolizes this harmony.

It is for no light reason that choir member and organist go through the drudgery of choir practice and the monotony of never-failing attendance upon the church services. In no part of the work of the church are loyalty and sacrifice more constantly needed. The choir member faces the exacting task unflinchingly because he loves his Lord and because he has in his heart precisely the same feeling which the Psalmist had when he cried out exultingly, "I will sing praises unto thee among the nations; for thy lovingkindness is great above the heavens" (Ps. 108:3).

Every lover of Christ wants to tell others about him, and the choir member serves loyally and willingly because he wants to use his special talent to express in music his appreciation for all that God and the church mean to him and those dear to him. This is a blessed form of ministry, quite as important as the sermon, and a fitting accompaniment to the preaching of God's word. No wonder that minister and choir meet together for a moment of prayer immediately before the service!

In many a local church one of the real problems is to induce a spirit of worship at the beginning of the service. Too often one hears personal conversation or thoughtless chatting in the narthex at the very time when the feeling of reverence for God should be paramount. An organist who has in his or her heart the spirit of worship can as if by magic create an atmosphere of reverence by the right type of instrumental music before the service begins.

Church music is doubly helpful because God is in it. When a worshiper is restless and jittery, a great calm comes over him as he sings:

Drop Thy still dews of quietness,
Till all our strivings cease;
Take from our souls the strain and stress,
And let our ordered lives confess
The beauty of Thy peace.[1]

When my mother lay dying, I thought of the great love which she had always had for Christ and of her loving service for him. It seemed to me then, more poignantly than ever before, that there is really no death and that Mother was simply returning to the Source of all life. As I held her frail body in my arms, these words which I had so often heard her sing came to me:

O Love that wilt not let me go,
I rest my weary soul in Thee;
I give Thee back the life I owe,
That in Thine ocean depths its flow
May richer, fuller be.[2]

The apostle Paul loved Jesus so much that he felt like a "captive" of his Lord. He was a "bond servant" who had no desire to be released. I doubt whether it would be possible for you and me to pray more earnestly for that kind of relationship than in the beautiful words of George Matheson:

Make me a captive, Lord,
And then I shall be free;
Force me to render up my sword,
And I shall conqueror be.
I sink in life's alarms
When by myself I stand;

[1] John Greenleaf Whittier, "Dear Lord and Father of Mankind."
[2] George Matheson.

Imprison me within Thine arms,
And strong shall be my hand.[3]

Even a military army appreciates the value of music as an inspiration to its soldiers. It is equally true of church music that it can inspire church people not only to worship but to action. "A Mighty Fortress Is Our God" and "Onward, Christian Soldiers" have a quality which inspires men and women to deep devotion and to action. If there is any criticism of the church today that is especially valid, it is that the church is too complacent, too quiescent. It may need something like the flaming soul of John Philip Sousa to galvanize it into action with music. For it is a fact, whether we like it or not, that we are "marching as to war." We need our church choirs and our choir leaders and our organists to give us the inspiration which only music can give.

There are sacred events in the life of every family when mere words fail utterly to express the depth of feeling and when only music can interpret the emotions. Such an event takes place when two souls are joined together in marriage. What words from the dictionary could give expression to a love that is so strong and so enduring that man and woman desire to give their hearts to each other for time and eternity?

The voices of angels are almost needed on such an occasion because the solemn contract into which the parties are entering is in reality a sacred covenant, for God is present at every wedding ceremony and the pledges made in the presence of witnesses are covenants, not only between the parties, but with God as an indispensable third party. When the binding words "I do" are spoken, and the representative of God places his seal upon the union, the only fitting accompaniment is "notes almost divine," and so a soft voice sings:

O perfect Love, all human thought transcending,
Lowly we kneel in prayer before thy throne,
That theirs may be the love which knows no ending,
Whom thou for evermore dost join in one.[4]

Yes, music is one of the lovely blessings of this life. And the process by which our ears catch it and register it on an appreciative brain is among life's miracles. In the souls of Bach, Beethoven, and Brahms were born beautiful melodies which are transmitted to our souls through in-

[3] Used by permission.
[4] Dorothy B. Gurney.

struments and voices almost divine. The noblest thoughts of which men are capable; the greatest beauty that the human soul can grasp; the most heavenly visions that poets can dream; the loveliest harmonies known to the universe—all these are brought to us through music. This is one of the many ways in which a loving heavenly Father speaks to his children and gives them a little bit of heaven.

CHAPTER 15

Our Lord and Master

"Nineteen wide centuries have come and gone, and today He is the centerpiece of the human race and the Leader of the columns of progress.

"I am far within the mark when I say that all the armies that ever marched, and all the navies that ever were built, and all the parliaments that ever sat, and all the kings that ever reigned, put together, have not affected the life of man upon this earth as powerfully as that one solitary life."

—Phillips Brooks

We love the church for its Saviour. Nearly two thousand years ago a little baby was born in Bethlehem. He proved to be the most wonderful baby ever born, for he was to change the whole course of the world, and he was to be loved and worshiped by millions through the centuries. What explains his great significance to mankind? Why did common people rejoice at the very word of his birth? Why did shepherds kneel in the hills to pray? Why did the Wise Men travel miles with their camels to bring him gifts?

The true significance of Jesus can be understood only by studying the background of his birth. He came to us as the Son of God. He was born into a world of great cruelty and suffering. It was a day when the strong persecuted the weak, even to the point of slavery. The great armies of Rome had overrun the civilized world and had brought all peoples under the cruel heel of the Roman emperor, who sent out his taxgatherers and his cruel judges and centurions into all parts of the known world to hold the people in subjection and to force them to pay tribute to Rome. If they did not pay, or could not pay, they were thrown into prison. The captives were consigned to a life of terror and misery as slaves rowing the Roman ships, chained to their places and whipped if they did not work to the point of exhaustion. Mothers saw their sons torn away and their daughters sold into slavery. Would not God intervene to end this misery?

It was under such circumstances that the Prince of Peace was born, in a humble manger in a barn in Bethlehem. Long had the poor millions of that land expected his birth, for it had been predicted in the book of Isaiah:

For unto us a child is born, unto us a son is given: and the government shall be upon his shoulder: and his name shall be called Wonderful, Counsellor, The mighty God, The everlasting Father, The Prince of Peace. Of the increase of his government and peace there shall be no end . . . to establish it with judgment and with justice from henceforth even for ever.

This quotation from the Bible was well known by all the people; they knew it by heart and repeated it over and over, hoping all the while that the child would really come. Every time a Jewish woman had a baby, she hoped and prayed that it would be a boy and that it would be the great Deliverer of whom Isaiah spoke. And so a people in gross misery and suffering cruel oppression looked forward with hope to the birth of their Saviour.

There could be no doubt that the child of Mary was the Saviour, for a bright star moved in the heavens, and God spoke to the Wise Men and told them to follow the star until it came to rest, and it did not rest until it was above the humble little place in Bethlehem. There lay a little babe who was to change the course of history, to make and remake empires, to cause kings and queens to fall, to bring inner peace to the hearts of millions.

The child grew up in an ordinary, poor neighborhood, just like many other children. But he showed a remarkable spiritual insight—so much so that at the age of twelve he was discussing religion with the priests in the Temple, and they marveled at his grasp.

As the child grew older, he began to teach in a most wonderful way. He taught doctrines that were radical, doctrines which no other man had ever dared to preach. "Never man spake like this man." To the leaders of Rome he dared to say: "Many that are first shall be last; and the last shall be first." For Jesus saw that true value lay not in power or in might, but in purity of heart. He shocked the rich, worldly men by reminding them that the poor widow dropping her little coin into the collection plate might be far ahead of them in the estimation of God. He shocked the man of pride by publicly declaring: "Blessed are the meek." And to the suffering and oppressed multitudes he preached the gospel that there is in every human heart a realm which belongs only to God, and which no man can touch. He taught them that men can be free even in slavery and that chains can be broken by the power of Almighty God. And so the poor flocked to him; the sick begged him to stand at their side; poor mothers who had lost their loved ones sought to touch the hem of his garment.

The Roman leaders, frightened by the new gospel, shouted, "That man is crazy! Crucify him, crucify him." And the priests who had been teaching and preaching a cold and empty religion, and who taught words rather than substance, called him a blasphemer and even insisted that he should be put to death because, they said, he was an enemy of the Jewish religion. After three years of active ministry he was condemned to death and taken to the top of a hill, where he was put on the cross by the men who feared him.

But he still lives. Even today his loving voice challenges a world at war. Even today he speaks out against dictatorship and exploitation. Even today he cries out against man's inhumanity to man. And people flock to churches to honor him, and after two thousand years they celebrate Christmas to rejoice in his birth.

And he is needed now just as much as he was needed in the days of old. For a loving God is still pleading with men to be pure and kind and unselfish. He is pleading with men not to be small, narrow, defeated beings, but to rise to the dignity of sons of God.

And so men of this day are still struggling toward the goal that is called the cross—the goal of love, of unselfishness, of a life purely and nobly lived. Millions of men, women, and children throughout the world are still pleading to be saved, and they see in Christ their only hope. And you and I, who bear his name, are trying in our small way to make good his pledge to a suffering world.

What are the things about Jesus Christ that mean most to the average layman and which laymen can apply in a practical way to their own lives? I would list them as follows:

His compassion. The word "compassion" comes from two Latin words meaning "suffering with." The love of Jesus Christ was the kind of love that was quite willing to suffer for and with any man. You and I must love more than we do.

His selflessness. He had no thought of personal gain, no concern for personal comfort, not even a pillow on which to lay his weary head. You and I are probably attaching too much importance to bank accounts and to the material side of life generally.

His boundless faith. The faith of our Lord did not waver when trouble came, not even in the shadow of the cross. You and I are too prone to be governed by fear.

His constant awareness of the Father. Just as a little child is always conscious of his father's love and care, so Jesus had a constant feeling that God was ever with him and sustaining him. So close was this relationship that the time came when Jesus could truthfully say: "I and my Father are one." Cannot you and I make God a more vital part of our lives?

His mercy. How much damage is done in our world by the cruelty of men and by what we laymen sometimes call the "hard-boiledness" of people! Jesus was always ready to forgive and to love, no matter how great the offense. In the Old Testament the emphasis was on punishment; in the New Testament the emphasis is on love. Do you and I have the reputation of being unusually kind and considerate?

His character. We laymen often wonder why we cannot attain the kind of relationship with God which we would like to have, when all the while the trouble is in our own characters—some disloyalty, some worship of the material, some uncontrolled desire. Jesus never sinned, although he was "tempted like as we are." He understood clearly what we laymen often fail to understand, that there can be no perfect communion with God as long as there is something wrong within us which we will not straighten out. Why not straighten it out now?

His courage. It was almost a case of Jesus against the great Roman Empire. But never did he bow his head to the emperor or fear the Roman legions. He stood unflinching before Pilate. At times we laymen seem to be afraid to take a stand on a moral issue, lest it prove unpopular. Jesus never cared about popularity. He thought only of being a true representative of his heavenly Father, and he never counted the effect upon his own fortunes. Are you and I willing to be unpopular for his sake?

His spiritual goal. Jesus always kept his eyes on the highest goal he knew—namely, complete obedience to his Father's will. His goal was the perfect life, the life lived in accordance with God's laws and with a complete disregard of self.

Here a parenthetical thought of some importance is justified. Jesus fervently believed that through faith men could live on a higher plane than the usual human level. Faith, he said, could even remove mountains. Often I have wondered why it is not possible for man, by right thinking and living, to reach higher spiritual goals than we have attained. Miracles can *still* be worked through faith. The trouble with most of us human beings is that we are content with a low level of faith. The miraculous power of Jesus is readily explained by a faith that was far superior to ours. We laymen should constantly pray for more faith.

His prayers. Prayer was intensely real to Jesus, so real that at times the perspiration that rolled from his brow while he was praying was like drops of blood. We laymen are entirely too casual with our praying. There can be no real communion with God except through earnest, and at times agonizing, prayer. What layman can say that he knows the meaning of agonizing prayer?

With tenderness and firmness Jesus has warned us laymen not to lay up for ourselves treasures upon earth, where moth and rust corrupt and where thieves break through and steal, but to lay up for ourselves treasures in heaven. We should pray daily that we may pay less attention to earthly treasures and more attention to the treasures that are eternal.

God sent Jesus to us to reveal himself to us. Jesus is not only the beautiful and perfect revelation of God, but he is the mediator between us and God, a mediator who willingly gave his life for us. It is not through our own merit that we are to be saved, but through the merit of Jesus Christ. It is through him and through him alone that we can be redeemed and our lost world saved.